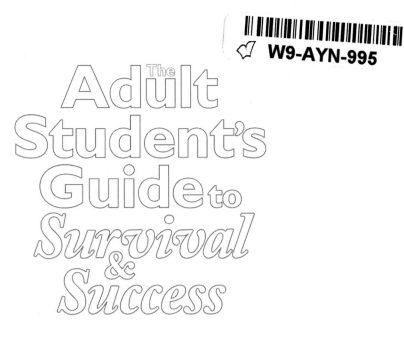
The Adult Student's Guide to *Survival & Success*

The Adult Student's Guide to Survival & Success
**Best Books Award Finalist ~
Education/Academic**
USA Book News 2008

Also:
Fall 2010 Selection of Black Expressions Book Club

also by Al Siebert:

The Resiliency Advantage: Master Change, Thrive Under Pressure and Bounce Back From Setbacks

The Survivor Personality: Why Some People Are Stronger, Smarter, and More Skillful at Handling Life's Difficulties . . . and How You Can Be, Too

also by Al Siebert and Mary Karr:

Teaching College Success to Adult Learners.
An instructor's manual to accompany *The Adult Student's Guide to Survival and Success, (6th ed.)*

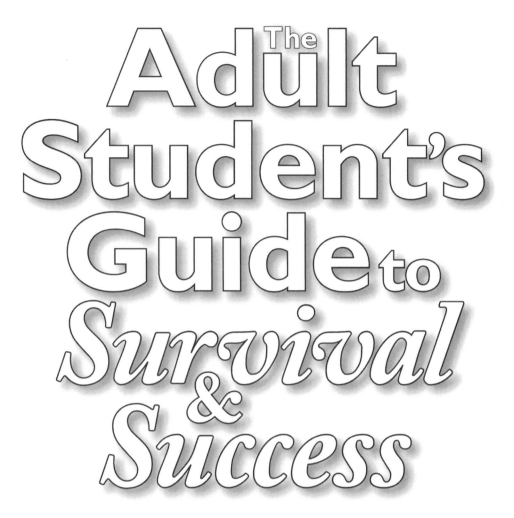

The Adult Student's Guide to Survival & Success

Sixth Edition

• Practical Psychology Press, Portland, Oregon •

Practical Psychology Press
P.O. Box 535
Portland, Oregon 97207-0535
www.PracticalPsychologyPress.com

Electronic versions available:
ISBNs: 978-0-944227-40-4 (PDF) / 978-0-944227-41-1 (Kindle)

Book/cover design/prepress by Kristin Pintarich, kpservices.us

Printed in the USA with vegetable-based ink on recycled-content stock by Thomson-Shore, Inc., a member of the Green Press Initiative.

15 14 13 12   10 9 8 7 6

Library of Congress Cataloging-in-Publication Data

Siebert, Al.
  The adult student's guide to survival & success / Al Siebert, Mary Karr.– 6th ed.
      p. cm.
  Includes bibliographical references and index.
  ISBN-13: 978-0-944227-38-1 (alk. paper)
  1. College student orientation–United States. 2. Adult college students–United States. 3. Study skills–United States. 4. Adult learning–United States. I. Karr, Mary, 1938- II. Title.
  LB2343.32.S556 2008
  378.1'98–dc22
                              2008007194

Contents

*To all students
with the courage and commitment
to pursue their dreams
and improve their lives.*

Foreword

If you feel nervous and have doubts about your ability to succeed in college, guess what. We felt the same way when we first started!

Al attended college as an army veteran. Mary started college when the youngest of her four children entered high school. After we each graduated, we decided to write a book about what we wish we'd had available when we first started. Our personal experiences shaped what we put into this book.

Since the first version of this book was published, thousands of adult students have found it extremely helpful. Many say they couldn't have made it through college without *The Adult Student's Guide*.

This revised sixth edition is loaded with practical information that will give you an advantage. It shows how to study effectively, pass tests, write excellent papers, and get high grades. It will help you deal with your concerns and more. It has many suggestions for handing the challenges that can block your progress. This new edition emphasizes how the skills you need for succeeding in college are the same skills most employers want today.

Mainly, we want to say that if you believe in yourself and take things one day at a time, you can get the education you want and find the financing you need. You have faced tough challenges before. You can survive the paper writing, test taking, and late night studying. With good effort and self monitoring you can succeed in college. We did, and we believe you can too!

Al Siebert, PhD
Mary Karr, MS   March, 2008

Chapter 1

Lots of Help Is Available

Did you know that over half of college students work while going to school?

How many services does your college provide to help you succeed?

Did you know that the abilities you use to succeed in college are the same abilities that employers look for?

What, in addition to a résumé and good grades, do employers look for?

Yes, You Can Succeed!

Your decision to go to college and then doing what it took to get registered means that you have a very good chance of completing your college program. Psychologists know this even though you may have some fears and doubts. The truth of this prediction can be found in your answers to the questions below.

Answer "yes" or "no" to these five questions:

Yes   No   During your elementary years in school were some of your classmates praised for being very bright?

Yes   No   When you were going to high school did you have to work hard to get passing grades?

Yes   No   When life hits you with difficult challenges do you feel optimistic about finding ways to overcome them?

Yes   No   Before you begin something difficult, do you think about what problems and barriers you might encounter and think of ways to avoid or overcome them?

Yes   No   When trying to cope with a difficulty, do you seek guidance from experienced people and experts about how to handle it well?

If you answered "yes" to most of the questions above, then the possibility that you will successfully complete your college program is very good. Here's why:

Research by psychologist Carol Dweck shows that many students who were praised for being very bright during their early years in school do not go on to achieve much career success. Because their early identity was to be one of the best and brightest, many of them become reluctant to take on new challenges or try new learning where they might not do well at first.

Dweck's research shows that students who were praised for getting passing grades by being persistent and sticking with difficult assignments often achieve more career success than their brighter classmates.

An accidental conversation during an airplane flight led psychologist Martin Seligman to conduct research about the importance of optimism in newly hired life-insurance sales agents. The insurance executive he talked with on the plane said that newly hired agents had to obtain high scores on the technical aspects of insurance, but many of them dropped out of the business after a year or two—which was an expensive business cost.

Seligman, famous for his research on "learned optimism" with depressed mental patients, set up an experiment. The results showed that if optimistic expectations were high in newly hired insurance agents, they had much more career success than new agents who had higher technical mastery but lower optimism scores.

David McClelland, a well-known Harvard psychologist, spent years trying to answer this question: "Why do some people achieve more career success than others?" His research—done with thousands of people in many countries—identified four factors. Successful people:

1. Daydream about what it will feel like to reach a goal that is meaningful for them.

2. They feel it is possible for them to reach the goal with good effort.

3. They spend time listing and anticipating how they will handle difficulties and problems that they may encounter.

4. They seek out experienced people and expert resources for guidance on how to succeed.

These research findings mean that you can succeed in college if you are willing to be persistent and work hard to obtain a passing grade in a course, feel optimistic about the results of your efforts, will take time to anticipate and deal with possible difficulties, and take advantage of all the expert resources available to you.

How *The Adult Student's Guide* Will Help You Reach Your Educational Goals

Every chapter in this book contains valuable information about how to succeed in college after you have been away from school for a while. It will show you how to succeed even if you have a family, work, have many responsibilities, and need time to spend with friends.

Most adult students take college courses to improve their job skills or career opportunities. *The Adult Student's Guide* contains many useful suggestions on how to be highly desirable to employers. *(Translation: hired quickly and paid well.)* Getting a diploma or a degree is not enough, however, in today's world. Employers in today's world of non-stop change are looking for people with college degrees who can prove that they:

+ can work well in teams
+ are self-motivated to keep learning new skills
+ have good communications skills
+ don't have negative attitudes
+ are dependable
+ have good computer skills
+ can work without a detailed job description
+ do not need constant supervision
+ provide excellent customer service
+ use common sense to solve problems
+ hold up well under pressure
+ are resilient and handle change well
+ do high-quality work

To help you develop abilities that will give you an advantage in the competition for a better job and help you reach higher levels of success on the job, we have included many suggestions on how to develop and *document* the abilities listed above. You will find, for example, guidelines on how to work in "learning teams," tips on how to improve communications skills, coaching on how to be highly resilient, and guidelines on how to develop a portfolio of accomplishments.

The Adult Student Online

If you are going to be employable in this age of technology, computer and internet skills are essential. *The Adult Student's Guide* gives you many opportunities to go online to practice and develop your internet skills.

The Adult Student's Guide is the first "student success" book designed to be interactive with its own website. Almost every chapter has additional information and updated resources at our AdultStudent.com website. You can access this site at www.AdultStudent.com. Throughout the book whenever you see the symbol ⌁ you will find a file or resource at the website.

Chapter Contents

The first half of the book covers academic challenges. It shows how you, as an adult student, can handle the challenges successfully. *The second half* covers non-academic challenges that can prevent you from succeeding in college and in your career if you do not handle them well.

Chapter 2 shows how to confront and overcome many fears and concerns of adult students. It answers most of the questions that adult students ask. (If your question isn't answered in the book, ask us at the Adult Student website!)

Chapter 3 shows how to make certain you are in the right educational program, get financing, and get oriented. Did you know that financial aid is available for adult students? Even part-time students? Chapter 3 (and the website) has information on how to finance your education.

Chapter 4 explains how to succeed in your courses. It shows how to find out what is required in each course, how to organize your notebooks, and how to take lecture notes.

Chapter 5 provides you with guidelines to online classes that are now being offered by most colleges. You will also learn how online classes differ from face-to-face classes.

Chapter 6 shows how to manage your time and how to study using an effective study method. Here you will learn how to reach a study goal, stop studying, and reward yourself. Self-motivated people must learn how to be self-stoppers!

Nervous about taking tests? **Chapter 7** shows how to prepare for all kinds of tests, so that you feel confident, less nervous, and score higher than you suspected you could. It also covers the type of critical thinking that earns high grades.

Term papers are always a challenge. In **Chapter 8** you will find efficient and effective ways to research and write papers that get top grades.

Chapter 9 shows how your way of learning may create conflicts between you and some instructors. It shows what to do about these mismatches and how to influence all kinds of instructors.

In **Chapter 10** you will find many practical tips on how to gain cooperation, support, and encouragement from your family, friends, and employers.

Most adult students work. **Chapter 11** shows how to combine working with taking college courses. Many employers offer special work schedules and reimbursement for courses completed. If you need to find a job to support yourself, or searching for a new career, we have many good suggestions at the Adult Student website.

Feeling pressured to get more work done in less time? **Chapter 12** explains effective ways to handle pressure, reduce stress, and develop inner strengths.

Could you succeed in a job that does not have a job description? **Chapter 13** shows how to be resilient in this world of non-stop change, bounce back from setbacks and gain strength from adversity.

At the end of most chapters you will find:

+ An **Action Review Checklist** for reviewing how well you are putting into action what the chapter covered.
+ **Learning Team and Support Group Activities** that will enhance your learning.

Create a Personal Support Group

Research into understanding why some people handle stress and difficult challenges better than others shows that the people who cope best have good support groups. Your college may provide a seminar for new students. These seminars increase your chances of succeeding in college.

If you can't fit a college success seminar into your schedule, we still want to encourage you to create your own support group or find a study partner. You'll be less lonely, develop good friendships, help each other through tough moments, and increase your chances of succeeding in college. You will find guidelines for creating a support group in Chapter 2.

Your Accomplishments Portfolio

You probably know that artists, models, and photographers have portfolios to show their work. Nowadays, because employers are overwhelmed by job applications, the applicants with the best chance of getting interviewed, in addition to a résumé, submit a one page summary outlining what they have documented in their portfolio of accomplishments.

Employment interviewers need your help! They appreciate and are impressed when someone has empathy for them. A one page summary of what is in your portfolio gets their attention.

Today's employers are looking for abilities not usually covered by traditional application forms and résumés. Throughout the book you will find activities you can use to help you document your ability to:

+ be a team member in a culturally diverse group,
+ communicate well,
+ problem-solve difficult challenges,
+ use critical thinking skills and good judgment,
+ research ideas,
+ use computers and software programs,
+ do consistently excellent work,
+ function well in constant change,
+ hold up under pressure keeping a good attitude,
+ reach your goals, and
+ are self-motivated to continuously develop new skills.

Many colleges provide their students with a portfolios website. With this arrangement, a potential employer can go online to examine accomplishments that you have documented at your college website.

To provide you with valuable guidelines we enlisted the help of Barbara Ritter, one of the pioneers in developing student portfolios. The steps she describes for creating an excellent portfolio would take too much space here, so we have placed her guidelines on how to create an accomplishments portfolio at our website.

↴ Look for the file "Your Accomplishments Portfolio" at www.AdultStudent.com

You are Special as a Student

Have you noticed that when you tell people about going to college they treat you differently? When Mary Karr started college she noticed an immediate change in how people treated her. She says:

> Before I started college, when my husband and I went to a party or social gathering, people would ask what I did. When I told them I was a housewife raising four children they'd say, "Oh," and start talking to someone else. On a scale from 1 to 100, I felt like I rated about a 3. After I enrolled, when people found out I was a college student, they'd say, "Oh!" I got treated like I had something important to say. My rating soared to the high nineties. The difference was fantastic! ~MK

Another student reported that he needed to change his working hours by half an hour to make a night class. He hesitated about approaching his supervisor, but finally spoke up. He asked for what he needed and explained why. His supervisor approved the change and from that day on his supervisor took a more personal interest in him and asked frequently about how school was going. Being a student can have some unexpected dividends!

The World Wants You to Succeed!

Going to college is an exciting challenge. It will take hard work and some sacrifices but the benefits are worth the effort. The main point to understand is that you are not alone. There are many people and many resources available to you. The world wants you to succeed in your effort to better yourself!

Chapter 2

Fears and Concerns: How to Confront and Overcome Them

Have you wondered if some of your fears about going to college are unrealistic?

Did you know that instructors enjoy teaching adult students? That adult students often get high grades?

In what ways do your life experiences give you an advantage in college?

What one activity will increase your chances of succeeding in college?

Facing Your Fears Takes Courage

In this book we will show you how thousands of people just like you found the courage to overcome their fears and succeed in college. We will show you how to develop the skills you need to increase your confidence. We will show you how to locate and use resources you never knew existed.

You may doubt your ability to succeed in college if you have not studied or taken tests for a long time, or if you have to work or have other responsibilities. It is possible, however, to be a successful college student and still handle other commitments.

You have overcome fears in the past by facing up to them and seeking information. You can do the same now. Before reading farther, take a minute to indicate how strong or weak your fear is about the following.

Strong—5   Moderately strong—4   Medium—3   Mild—2   Weak—1

1. __ I won't be able to learn quickly, my brain is rusty.
2. __ I don't think I can do college level math.
3. __ The thought of taking tests in college worries me.
4. __ I won't be able to compete with younger students.
5. __ I won't be able to study well.
6. __ I don't have a computer or internet access.
7. __ I don't know how to use computers like the kids do.
8. __ Instructors might dislike older students.
9. __ I won't fit in.
10. __ I can't afford college.
11. __ I can't work and study and raise a family.
12. __ My family will feel neglected.
13. __ People in my life will try to sabotage my efforts.
14. __ Going part-time will take me too long.

Common Fears and Concerns of Adult Students

If your total score from the above list is over 45 you definitely need to look through the following list of fears and concerns. They are typically felt and experienced by most adult students starting college. And like many fears you have experienced in your life, many of these fears are not realistic either.

I haven't studied in years. I'm out of practice. My brain feels rusty.

Reality: There is no evidence that older students can't learn or remember as well as younger students. This book will show you how to take notes, remember information from lectures and texts, and pass tests as well as any younger student.

I'm not sure I can read, write, or do math well enough to succeed in my college courses.

Reality: The college will give you a free assessment of your skill levels to advise you what courses are best suited for you. If you need brush-up courses, they are available.

─\᷍⟋─ For more information see the section on Learning Disabilities at our website: AdultStudent.com

I'm worried about taking tests. Is there a way to reduce my nervousness without taking a tranquilizer?

Reality: Test anxiety is reduced in students who follow the guidelines in the chapters ahead. And remember, there is plenty of extra help available to show you how to reduce your anxieties about taking tests. College counseling and study skills centers provide help for students who need to learn techniques of test taking. Ask around.

I'll feel like a misfit, like an outsider in a strange world. I won't fit in.

Reality: The number of adult students on campus has grown in the last decades. Students over the age of 25 make up approximately 39% of total student population across the nation as opposed to 28% in 1970, and the numbers continue to rise. The traditional student, fresh from high school, dependent on family for financial support, and holding no more than a part-time job accounts for only 27% of college enrollees. Truth is, the faculty, administrators, and students will be more friendly and helpful than you might imagine. Many younger students enjoy having older friends from whom they can learn and exchange views and experiences. Making cross-generational friends can be one of the most rewarding parts of your educational experience. Besides, remind yourself that your tax dollars may have helped build the place. You have a right to be there.

I was so nervous the first day of classes that I arrived at school 45 minutes ahead of the 9:00 class time. It was OK though, because I needed the time to keep running into the rest room—bladders seem so insistent sometimes. As I walked into the room for my first class I realized that my legs were shaking so hard I could barely walk. Fortunately, the front seat nearest the door was available so I quickly sat down. I tried to remain calm, but I knew I was trembling—my hands just wouldn't stop. After a very long time, the teacher came in and was ready to start the class. The first thing I noticed was how young she was and I thought to myself that school was going to be harder than I had imagined because how could this very young woman (she looked like a student herself) ever understand someone my age. Then I noticed that her legs were shaking! *She was nervous! Wonderful!* My day changed and was grand from then on. Oh yes—I also found out that she was a graduate teaching assistant and that she was very sympathetic to all students. ~ MK

I won't be able to compete. Only a few smart students receive high grades.

Reality: Times have changed! In the past many instructors graded "on the curve." They gave high marks to the few students who scored better than others in the class. Now, however, most instructors grade students on how much learning they accomplish during a course. Further, in many courses you will work on team projects with other students. This means that you and other students work together to master the material and all get excellent grades.

> Don't be embarrassed if you can't do everything quickly.
> Don't try to compete with the young—compete with yourself.
> —*Eva Corazon Fernando-Lumba, age 78*
> (*Chosen by her classmates to be the class speaker at commencement.*)

Instructors won't like having an older student in class.

Reality: Instructors enjoy adult students. They welcome the life experience and critical thinking skills that older students offer to a class. They expect to find communication is easier with you. Returning students are frequently more motivated to learn and pay closer attention to the instructor. Studies show older students tend to get better grades than younger students.

I can't afford four years of college.

Reality: Most students qualify for some sort of financial aid, including adult students. This may be in the form of scholarships, loans, grants, or employer reimbursements. And did you know that programs now exist where you can earn college credit for working? We will cover this in more detail in Chapter 3. College administrators and counselors are aware of the financial dilemmas facing returning students and will assist you in obtaining financial help. (See also Resources and Suggested Readings.)

I have young children, but I can't afford the cost of child care. How can I attend classes with children to raise?

Reality: Colleges are doing much to assist people who have children. There are child-care referral services at many colleges and women's resource centers. Many campuses offer low-cost child-care services for students. Many student parents trade child-care time with other students. To work out a cooperative schedule one student takes day classes, the other night time or weekend classes. Some student parents vary days of the week with one taking classes on Monday, Wednesday, Friday, the other on Tuesdays and Thursdays.

I cannot attend full-time. It is hard to imagine all the years it will take to get a college degree.

Reality: To fulfill your dream of getting an education, start now! Once you become adjusted to being a student and gain confidence, you will probably be able to take more courses each term. Or you might consider a shorter program. Many colleges offer two-year programs for people training for specific careers such as a dietician or an associate degree in nursing. Regardless of the program you take, most students say their college careers go much faster than they thought possible.

My friends and family will suffer if I have to spend lots of time with schoolwork and my partner may feel threatened by my attempt to improve myself?

    Reality: You will probably be surprised at how much your family and friends will support you in your new role as a student. Explain to them why you need to return to school. Show how your success will benefit all of you. Give them a chance and they will probably be very encouraging. Chapter 10 has a number of practical suggestions.

I have a heavy load at work. I have too many pressures to take college courses.

    Reality: Did you know that many college courses are offered one evening a week, or even online? If you are willing to give up one evening a week, or spend time at a computer, you can take a college course. Employers are often willing to adjust workloads for employees in college, see Chapter 10. The time management tips in Chapter 6 will help. Chapter 5 will give suggestions for online classes. For guidelines on dealing with multiple pressures, read Chapter 12. The solution is to decide what you want in life and go for it.

If I become a student, I'll never have time for my family, friends, or outside interests. I can't take courses, study, and still have time for anything else.

    Reality: It is true that you won't be able to do everything you did before and also be a college student. You will have to make some changes. But many thousands of people have gone to college while working and maintaining active personal lives. You are no different. Look ahead to chapter 10 for practical suggestions. Take advantage of all the tips and examples. When you follow all the guidelines for succeeding in college, you'll do just fine and have time for other important things as well.

> I finally dragged myself over to the community college and took two courses. I was scared to death. I had been at war, in police riots, and a fire fighter and that was all right. But, now I'm going to this college and I'm scared to death. I literally

had stomach cramps—got physically sick. I really don't know why I was scared. I had no idea...no reason...it had nothing to do with anything...there was no consequence to pay...I could have gone over there, flunked out, and nothing would have happened. I would still have been a lieutenant in the fire department. Nothing would have changed. As it turned out, I left there with a 4.0 after taking four courses. But, when I first went through the door, I was dying. —Bob DePrato

Anything is Possible...

As you can see, there are ways to handle your concerns about being a college student. Many fears disappear when you confront them. As other fears or concerns develop, here are the steps to follow:

1. First identify exactly what your fear or concern is. Write it down or describe it to someone. Then ask, "Is my worry based on rumors, or opinions, or is it a result of known facts?"

2. To cope with problems or difficulties that might occur, ask other adult college students about their experiences. Find out if your fears are real.

3. With specific, realistic problems, talk to an academic advisor or a college counselor. They will help you develop a realistic plan of action coping with the problem. Remember: *Don't be afraid to ask for help!*

Let Us Know!

⌁ Do you have other concerns? Suggestions for other students? Please let us know at our Adult Student website: www.AdultStudent.com.

Learning Teams and Personal Support Groups

Since businesses expect employees to work in teams, many instructors also require you to work on team projects and give group reports. In classes with team projects, the student teams are often arbitrarily assigned. They are usually given access to an online group-project site. If your instructor does not assign learning teams, you can create one (or more) of your own!

Get together with other new students who would like to discuss various college issues (personal support group) or specific coursework (learning team). These days you have options if a face-to-face meeting doesn't fit in with your group's busy schedule. You can meet online with a blog or through email, or at a networking site like Facebook.com or LinkedIn.com. Many colleges have similar websites that allow groups to form and connect privately like the classroom group-project sites. Creating a personal support group and issue-specific learning teams is the single most effective thing you can do to help assure your success in college.

If your group decides to meet face-to-face, then the following suggestions will help keep the group on track.

Learning Team and Support Group Hints for Success

Why should we form a support group rather than just getting together with a couple of people whenever we can?

Well, you've heard about the road that is paved with good intentions. Getting together is fine for providing a relaxed social meeting, but after the first couple of weeks busy people just don't have time to chat for more than a few minutes. By committing yourself and others to a set time and place and agenda for what you are going to discuss, everyone will be more likely to continue to participate. An effective support group will provide each member with results that helps you be successful in your college classes.

Does our support group need a group leader?

Probably not in a formal sense, but groups fall apart quickly when no one is responsible for some of the tasks. One way to run a support group is to have everyone be the leader for a week or a month. That person should have specific responsibilities for his/her time of leadership. Some leader responsibilities are:

+ Inform everyone of the meeting day and time
+ Start meetings on time
+ Introduce discussion topics
+ Keep discussions on track

- ✦ Set day and time for next meeting
- ✦ Set agenda for next meeting

What about someone to act as recorder?

It's useful to have written notes or a computer record of what was discussed. Also, if someone misses one meeting, the discussion notes will be useful. As with the group leader job, the job of note-taker could rotate each week or month.

How often should we meet?

You decide that. Once a week works best for most adult students. Meeting more often can get complicated as the demands of classes start to increase. Every two weeks might work, but meeting less frequently will lose the personal continuity that regular meetings provide.

Is there anything else we should do?

You should make sure to know how to contact everyone. Exchange phone numbers and email addresses. Find out the preferred way to contact each person.

You may want to set up a "Yahoo" mailing list group or put your group members' emails into a mailing list as your software allows. Learn about the "bcc" field in your email program. This field allows you to send a copy to the list, but keeps the names and email addresses of the other participants hidden. To use this, put your own name in the "To" field and the rest of the list in the "bcc" field. You will still get an error message if there is a problem with an individual's email. Be alert to whether you are replying to the whole group or just one person and choose the best option as each situation necessitates. Posting to the group what is better sent as a personal conversation is a time waster for everyone. It sometimes takes a little practice to learn the difference and get it right, so don't sweat it at first.

Learning Team and Support Group Activities

1. Talk with each other about your fears and concerns. Then discuss how you can overcome or eliminate the fears and barriers. Keep in mind that some problems can't be eliminated, but it helps to talk with people who understand.

2. Discuss the difference between academic and non-academic challenges that concern you. Write your own list, then develop a plan for dealing with each item on your list.

3. Ask each other about difficult challenges that you've dealt with in the past. Ask for examples of being resilient and how you were strengthened and become more self-confident by rough experiences. These memories will help remind you that you have the inner strength to cope well and be made stronger and better by adversity.

4. Discuss the difference between having a high IQ and being "emotionally intelligent." Why is emotional intelligence important in life? For more information on emotional intelligence, see the AdultStudent.com website.

Chapter 3

How to Choose Your Program, Get Financial Help, and Become Oriented

What are three ways you can turn some of your acquired job and life skills into college credit?

Did you know you can probably get financial aid if you need it?

Where can you inquire about financial assistance?

How do you apply for federal financial aid?

Where do you go with questions about class schedules, transportation, health services, or security?

Choosing a Program That Calls to You

Find Out What Courses Are the Path to Your Vocation

Do you know what the word "vocation" means? It means "a calling." It is a path with heart. It is "work" you enjoy doing so much that you are delighted to be paid for doing it. People who have found their "vocation" are generally more motivated than people taking courses simply to get a college degree.

Take time to look carefully through the college catalog. List the courses you will have to take to graduate. Even if you haven't settled upon a degree field yet, you will have to take several general education courses required of all students in a degree program. The college catalog describes all the courses offered and explains which ones you will be required to take if you want to receive a degree or certificate. Read the requirements carefully.

The college catalog is a kind of contract. The college agrees to award you a degree if you do all the required work as indicated in the catalog in force during your initial enrollment into degree course work. Keep a copy for future reference.

If a course sounds interesting, check to see if you have to take a prerequisite course before taking it. A *prerequisite* course is one that students must take and complete before they can get into a more advanced course.

Some courses are so popular there are many sections scheduled during a day with different instructors. If you have a choice, find out which instructors other students recommend and why they recommend them. Keep in mind, however, that an easy teacher may not be the best for your future. You are in college to get a solid education, not just a degree.

Once you know the courses you want, look at the schedule of classes. The *schedule* will tell you the time, location, and instructor for each course. If you do not find that a course you want is available at this time, contact the department. Ask the secretary when the course you want will be offered next and who will teach it. Department secretaries are a gold mine of information. Not every course is offered every term or semester, so it might be practical to outline a two-year schedule for yourself at this time.

If you live in an area with several public colleges, you might find it more convenient to be enrolled at one college, but take a course at another if the course is offered at a better time, for a lower cost, or not offered at your main campus. So many college students do this, there is now a name for it: "swirling." It is legal to do, and in most cases with state-funded schools, a basic course such as introduction to sociology must be accepted for full credit when transferred back to your primary college.

You and your academic advisor will need to decide how many courses and credit hours you should take. Full-time students usually take four to five classes per quarter, or about three where on semesters. If you take two or three courses for less than about 12 credit hours, you may be considered a part-time student, depending on the college. Note that being enrolled part-time versus full-time can affect your eligibility for financial aid.

Certificate and Degree Choices

Community colleges offer *vocational certificate* programs in such fields as food services, nursing, dental assistant, computer science, television production, software specialist, internet associate, and hotel hospitality services.

Community colleges also offer *Associate Degree* programs that take about two years to complete as a full-time student. Most courses in these Associate Degree programs will be accepted by your state's four-year colleges, and you may be able to waive some course requirements if you are looking to transfer to pursue a bachelor's degree.

Enrollment at a four year college or university can lead to the following academic degrees:

Bachelor of Arts (BA)—Earned in a four year program emphasizing humanities, language, and arts courses.

Bachelor of Science (BS)—Earned in a four year program emphasizing science courses that include mathematics and statistics.

Master's degree (MA, MS, MEd)—Earned after the BA or BS, taking approximately two years of courses in arts or science and writing and defending a thesis.

Doctorates: Philosophy (PhD), Education (EdD), Psychology (PsyD), etc.—Usually earned after the master's degree with advanced, graduate level seminar work and a doctoral thesis based on original research.

Classroom Alternatives: Internet and Television-Based Courses

University and College Sites: College instructors use computers and the internet to aid in the teaching of their courses. The instructor may post course outlines, notes, supplemental materials, self-tests, and other aids that can assist with student learning at the college website. Some of these may be accessible to the public or to students only through the use of a logon and password. As a student, you can access these pages from your home computer or from computers on campus. Most local libraries also have computers for your use if you do not have your own.

Online Courses: Online courses are conducted by instructors, but instead of going to a classroom on campus you "go to class" using a computer and your instructor teaches the class using his or her computer. An online class allows the instructor and students to log on, "arrive," and "leave" at times that fit their individual time schedules. Usually, assignments, discussions, etc., are to be completed by a specific time each week. One student may visit class and post assignments at 3:15 AM, while others are in and out all through the day and evening. (See Chapter 5 for more about online learning.)

Telecourses: Most colleges have telecourse studios where an instructor at the college teaches a class to a group of students in a telecourse studio somewhere else. Telecourses are like regular classrooms. They are "real time." Everyone is in class at the same time. The instructor will use the television broadcast or internet links to see and hear students, and students will watch the instructor on a TV screen or monitor. Discussions will include students at all the locations.

Get Credit Without Taking Class

Prior Learning Assessment (PLA) Credits. Did you know you can receive college credit for learning you have acquired through a variety of experiences? If you ran your own business, for example, and now wish to earn a business degree, PLA credit may be a possibility for you. Some colleges and universities offer prior learning assessment credits or other credits for life and work experience.

Educational institutions offering these credits usually have workshops to help you describe and document your learning. Credit can be earned for more than paid work experience. Some students have used travel, volunteer work, self-directed study, and community activities as a basis for PLA credit. PLA programs will not all be alike. Colleges set their own requirements for the program, so you will want to find out what the specifics are in your field of study at your school.

A lot of writing and verification is required, but you may be rich in life experience and able to qualify for official college credit. There are many rewards that come from earning credit for prior learning including academic recognition and validation of just how much you have learned in life, enhancing your research and writing skills, and a significant savings in time and money. Credits must be paid for, but when the push of time and experience is on your side, it is an option to consider. The savings is realized in an overall shorter time on campus.

As an evaluator of PLA communication essays for my college, I have been fascinated with the life experiences of students. Many enter the program feeling unsure of how their experiences can be used for academic credit. At my school, students work with a mentor while working on essays. By the time the essays get to me, students have polished their writing and have documented how they gained the experience. I am pleased when I can award credit to students for the learning they have done before entering college. ~ MK

College Level Examination Program (CLEP). This testing program, administered by the College Board allows you to show proficiency in a subject based on a test. There are about 35 subjects ranging from business law to German. Since each of the nearly 3000 colleges handle CLEP scores differently, and not all accept every test subject, ask your college advisor about these tests and how to arrange for them. Some information is available online. The subjects may have been studied in an advance course in high school, special training at work, or gained through life experience.

The CLEP score subjects will be recorded on your transcript and count as credit toward graduation. You do not have to pay the college for the credits recorded, but there may be a test administration fee of about $15 dollars plus the College Board charges about $70 for taking the test. Military veterans and eligible civilian support personnel can apply for VA reimbursement.

Challenging Courses. A third way to get college credit without taking courses is to challenge introductory level courses at the college. A more comprehensive description of the course work can be seen in a "course content guide" often available through the department secretary. If you believe you already know a subject quite well, and the college allows, you can arrange to take the final examination in a course to see if you can pass it. If you do, you can get credit for the course by paying the normal registration fee. Keep in mind, however, that you may miss out on a valuable foundation for more advanced courses in the subject.

Buy Your Textbooks Early

After you have registered, go to the bookstore and purchase the required textbooks for your courses. In the bookstore each shelf will list the instructor and course that the books are for.

Do not wait until after the first class meeting to buy your books because the bookstore may not have ordered enough books for everyone. They generally expect some students to drop the course and bring books back for a refund, but you can't count on this.

If you buy a used textbook, or textbooks online, pay close attention to which edition it is. Purchase only the most recent edition of a textbook. The instructor will not approve of your using a used second edition of a textbook when the third edition is now the one he or she uses. It also may haunt you on tests as facts and figures you study may not be the correct ones.

When you purchase your textbooks keep your receipts and do not put your name in your books, at least not right away. If for any reason the course is cancelled or you do not want to stay in it, you can sell your books back to the bookstore for a full refund within a certain time limit.

Courses Can Be Dropped

If, after attending the first or second class in a course you realize you've made a serious mistake, then consider dropping the class or transferring to another course. Remember, though, *it is normal to feel somewhat overwhelmed by a course at first.* Talk to the instructor or check with an advisor before dropping. If you drop a course early, most of your money may be refunded.

Financial Assistance is Available From Many Sources

Financial help can be obtained from federal and state aid programs, scholarships, gifts, grants, and loans. This assistance can cover the difference between what you can afford to pay and what it will cost you to go to college. Under federal and state aid programs all families and individuals are treated equally by a standardized evaluation of how much you and/or your family can afford to pay. Age is not a consideration.

Visit Your College Financial Aid Office

The office for financial aid has information about many sources of money for college students. Filling out the application forms can take time, but the effort can pay off. If the forms appear overwhelming don't give up! The financial aid personnel will lead you through the forms step-by-step if necessary, and will give you current and exact information for your institution. Additionally, some colleges offer an online tutorial or video that takes you through the application process.

You apply for all federal grants and loans using the Free Application for Federal Student Aid (FAFSA) that comes out each January for the academic year beginning the following fall. It may be mailed to you on request, or found online at www.fafsa.ed.gov. Submit the completed application as soon as possible because funds are often distributed on a first come, first served basis. Even if you qualify you will not get any funds if the school's allocated money for a certain loan program is used up. Download the provided worksheets and practice with this year's version.

Prepare to fill out the financial forms by outlining a rough budget of your expenses for the year. Your expenses will include:

tuition and fees, books and supplies, room and board, transportation, and personal expenses. To get a handle on what your needs may be, use online calculators for college costs and Estimated Family Contribution such as the one available from the College Board: http://apps.collegeboard.com/fincalc/efc_welcome.jsp

Scholarships are Available for Nearly Everyone

Scholarships are set up for many student groups, not just the exceptionally bright ones. Many funds are available for minorities, veterans, displaced homemakers, women over a certain age, single parents on social security, and students with special talents or career objectives. Scholarships do not have to be repaid.

To search for scholarships, start with FinAid.com. This site will search thousands of scholarships looking for potential matches.

Your success in finding free money is only limited to your willingness to "do your homework," follow through, and fill out as many application forms as you can. The first ones are the hardest, from there, you can draw upon what you've already submitted to fill out the rest. Be creative in tailoring each application to the specific scholarship as much as possible. Some funds are available from unlikely sources such as local service clubs and professional associations, for example. Applying for all for them—even ones you're not qualified for—can make the difference in finding funds. Scholarships that get no applicants go unawarded, so you may as well put yourself on the list of possible candidates!

Government Aid Comes in Many Forms

Scholarships are only one form of aid or financial support offered to students. The US Department of Education (DOE) as well as states and individual colleges make funds available to college students through a number of student grant and loan programs. The internet can be a big help in accessing data for funds, as well as visiting on-campus financial aid offices. A good reference is the DOE publication, *Funding Education Beyond High School.*

A *grant* is an outright gift. It does not have to be repaid. Financial aid can also be in the form of reduced tuition. At some colleges, students without funds may qualify for a reduction in tuition and fees. Many top-tier and private colleges with sizable endowments are reducing fees across the board for low-income students.

You can apply for federal loans and grants through the college or directly to the DOE using the FAFSA as discussed above. No longer are federal loans offered through private lending institutions. One application applies for all these programs:

Pell Grants (also known as Basic Educational Opportunity Grants) can range from $600 to $5,550 (the annual limit is now tied to the Consumer Price Index and is expected to be nearly $6,000 for the 2017-8 school year) for the first year for an undergraduate enrolled full-time, with an average award near $2,500. Reduced funds are available for students who can only enroll part-time. No payback is needed when your courses are successfully completed.

Federal Supplemental Educational Opportunity Grants vary a great deal with each institution. Unlike Pell Grants, the amount of FSEOGs you receive depends not only on your financial need but also on the amount of other aid you get and the availability of funds at your school. A community college may provide several hundred dollars based on your need while a university or private college may have up to $4,000 a year available. No repayment is required on completion of course work.

Subsidized and Non-Subsidized Loans. These loans must be paid back if you stop attending college at least half-time for six months. If the loan is subsidized, the federal government pays the interest on it until you start making payments. If non-subsidized, your interest begins to accrue from the first monetary disbursement. Recently, the federal government has granted partial to full cancellations and deferments in several loan categories in exchange for a one- to five-year full-time teaching placement at a school with a teacher shortage or low-income status. Most common placements are in science, math, special education, and foreign language instruction at rural or inner city schools.

Stafford/Ford Loans are federal student loans and vary according to need and institution. For independent students a high-cost college may loan up to $7,500 the first and second years and $10,500 in subsequent years up to a total of $46,000. Colleges with lower costs will have lower maximum loan limits.

Perkins Loans (also known as National Direct Student Loans) vary according to need and institution. Colleges can run out of funds so get your application in early. Funds awarded can change from year to year. Here too, borrowers who undertake certain public, military, or teaching service employment are eligible to have all or part of their loans cancelled.

Other federal programs include federal work study; the TRIO program for first-generation college students, low-income, or disabled Americans; and a multitude of scholarships and grants available for specific fields of study, such as the National SMART and TEACH grants. Each institution is different, so contact your college's financial aid office for the specific funding opportunities they offer and how to apply for them.

If you are a veteran, you probably know about your GI benefits provided by the federal government, but did you know that educational benefits may also be provided by your state? The office of financial aid at your college can tell you if you qualify.

Income-Based Repayment (IBR). With most loans, a payment schedule is available; the entire loan does not come due at once. A new federal program, IBR is intended to cap your payment of federal loans at an affordable level based on family size and income. Note that these adjustments will most likely lengthen the term of loan repayment, and increase the actual amount of interest you pay.

Private/Non-Government-Subsidized Loans. Additional options for funding may come from private loans and low- or no-interest charity loans. Private loans come from individuals you may or may not know, organizations, companies, and private lenders. Charity loans are awarded by charitable foundations, non-profit and service organizations. Private and charitable lenders will often look at different criteria than federal lenders. You will have to apply to each lender individually as private loans are generally not processed through the college's financial aid office. Some places on the web to start looking are: VirginMoneyUS.com, FoundationCenter.org, Prosper.com, BankRate.com, and Zopa.com.

⎯⋏⎯ See the AdultStudent.com website for links to funding sources, latest limits, tips, and application forms.

Beware! "Student Loan Scam"

In 2007, the student loan industry came under fire for questionable lending practices. Both public and private loan companies along with campus financial aid offices engaging in deceptive marketing campaigns, staffing practices, and kickbacks. The problem? These "preferred" lenders and co-opted financial aid offices did not always offer the most favorable loan packages for the student, and in some cases, offered high risk, high rate "opportunity loans" to students with little or no credit history. Stephen Burd, fellow at the New America Foundation reports:

> Only 32 lenders hold 90% of the [student] loan volume. What's more, the Education Department has found that at about 300 colleges, one lender controls 99% of the loan volume — essentially holding a monopoly on those campuses.

The fallout for you, the student, is the Student Loan Sunshine Act which makes things safer by enacting additional oversight by the federal government, disclosure requirements, and an industry "code of conduct" agreement. However, this doesn't mean you are completely protected. Watch for schools that still have only one, two, or a few preferred lenders. They are required to let you have access to any lender of your choice, not just their preferred ones.

Funding Strategies

Some experts suggest "maxing out" your federally subsidized loans before looking to the private market. However, using more than one lender to finance your education can lead to more options for repayment. Remember, you don't *have* to get your funding through the school's financial aid office.

If your program is not unique to your school, it can be useful to inquire at different colleges to see where you can get the best financial aid package. The offers will vary. Also, ask again closer to your enrollment date if any funds have become available due to other students choosing to go elsewhere. In addition, if you are looking for a four-year degree, consider taking some (or all) of the lower division required classes through a local community college and transferring the credits. Costs savings can be 80% or more per course.

A "gotcha" you need to explore is a school's accreditation status. Federal aid is not awarded to non-accredited schools. While most four-year universities and state or regional community and junior colleges are accredited, many less-than-two-year profes-sional schools are not. You can check your school's status at: www.ope.ed.gov/accreditation/

Even the Internal Revenue Service May Help

An indirect savings you may be eligible to receive include federal tax credits for tuition and fees: the Hope, American Opportunity, or Lifetime Learning credits. The Hope Credit has been modified and, for most tax payers, is now known as the American Opportu-nity Tax Credit (AOC). It provides up to $2,500 per year for the first four years of post-secondary education. Currently, if you choose to attend a college in a Midwestern disaster area, the Hope Credit is still available for the first two years, and you may be eligible for up to $3,600 per year, but may change or go away at any time. The Lifetime Learning Credit (LLC) provides 20% of costs up to $1,000 a year and can be used at any time, even for a single course. You can only take one of these credits per year, so start with the Hope Credit if you qualify, then AOC, then LLC. See *IRS Publication 970 "Tax Benefits for Education"* for specific information.

Employer Reimbursement

Many employers reimburse employees for their tuition after a college course is completed. Sometimes the course work must be directly related to the job. Other employers pay for all classes leading to a degree. Some unions have negotiated for significant academic benefits so their members can increase their job skills. In any case, if you work while going to college, it is worth checking with your employer directly. You may also be able to make spe-cial arrangements to take time off from work or to take your class online at your work site. Many larger companies bring college courses to the work site. You won't know if you don't ask.

Jobs On and Off Campus

Another source of funds is through student employment programs. More information can be found in Chapter 11. There are many jobs available for students who need income. The main point is that many possibilities exist for helping college students get an educa-tion. Don't rule yourself out without checking. Inquire!

Explore Your New College Community

What do you do when you move into a new community? You explore. You don't passively sit and wait for someone to come knocking on your door with brochures about local businesses and services. Not at all. You go around visiting stores, businesses, and shopping centers in the area. You ask people for directions. You locate places that provide important services. You talk with neighbors to find out which places are best and which ones to avoid. Take time to get acquainted with your school in the same way that you would be curious about a new community you move into. Be active and curious, not passive or timid. Learn about the many resources and services available to you. You will feel comfortable about coming to campus more quickly, and the more you locate and use resources, the more successful you will be.

Starting college is like moving into a new community. The orientation leaders will give you stacks of information about college facilities and services available to you, but no matter how complete they are, your own active exploring around campus will be more useful to you.

⌁ Our website has a file listing support services and facilities available at most colleges. Use it as a basic checklist of places to visit: www.AdultStudent.com

If possible, visit every service or facility to get acquainted. Introduce yourself to staff members and ask what help they provide students. Don't be shy! All the college support services exist to help students like you succeed and graduate. Make every effort to take the guided orientation tour provided by the college. The tour leader will answer any questions you have.

Be sure to pick up a copy of the college newspaper. It is free, and the first edition of the new school year will be loaded with information for new students.

The more quickly you become familiar with the college campus, the more quickly you will feel comfortable in this new community and be able to focus on your studies.

➤ *REMEMBER: The entire school exists to help you get the education you want! Take advantage of what it has to offer.*

Locate Your Classrooms

Once you know which courses you will be taking, go find the rooms where each of your classes will meet. Learn where each classroom is located and how you'll get from one room to the next. The day classes start, trying to find your way around campus can be hectic!

Action Review Checklist: Becoming Oriented

◇ Have I read through the college catalog?

◇ Do I have specific courses in mind that I want to take?

◇ Have I found out if I need to apply for admission?

◇ Have I checked with the financial aid office to find out about my eligibility for financial assistance?

◇ Have I inquired about educational benefits or support from my employer?

◇ Do I know how to register for the courses I want?

◇ Do I know where my classrooms are located?

◇ Have I explored the campus to find out what is available to students?

◇ Do I feel well oriented to the college?

Learning Team and Support Group Activities

1. Talk about what difficulties you encountered trying to get registered for courses. Talk about the courses you plan to take. Help each other look into ways to tailor your selection of courses to fit your unique interests and needs. Be frank with each other about your financial needs. Someone in your group may know of a way to get extra financial help.

2. Ask each other about specific resources in and around your school. What services, businesses and food establishments have others found for both school and leisure?

Chapter 4

Actions That Lead to Success in College

Can you explain how ordinary people succeed as college students?

What does it means to view college as a learning environment?

How do you take good lecture notes?

What is the effect of self-esteem on success in college?

I'm a single parent, low-income, first generation student and a black female. I'm surely one that sociologists would label as disadvantaged. But with the assistance of the special services program and my desire, my commitment and strong will to distance myself from the labels and statistics, I have achieved my goal of completing college.

—Edna Mae Pitman
TRIO Achiever Award Winner
(One of 26 college students in the nation selected by the National Council of Educational Opportunity Association from more than 425,000 students in TRIO programs.)

Success in Each Course Leads to Success in College

You can do well in college without being an ideal student. Success comes from being motivated to succeed and doing the things that lead to success in your courses. Thousands of ordinary people who are nervous, have doubts, and who didn't stand out in high school do very well in college.

Research into student success shows that students who do consistently well in the courses they take are those who:

+ find out at the first class meeting when all the tests will be held and when papers or projects are due.
+ attend all classes.
+ prepare for each class in advance.
+ ask several good questions during class.
+ take good lecture notes.
+ organize their time well.
+ study regularly.
+ set specific study goals each time they study.
+ hand in coursework on time.
+ prepare for tests by writing practice tests.
+ stop studying when they reach their study goals.
+ work well with other students on group projects.

In addition, successful students are self-motivated, appreciate and encourage other students, have strong self-esteem and self-confidence, develop good study habits, and associate with other successful students. More about this later.

Find Out What is Required

Successful students actively determine the requirements for each course. During the first lecture they get answers to these key questions:

✦ Which chapters in the textbook will be covered?

✦ When will the exams be given? is there a syllabus (schedule)?

✦ What material will each exam cover?

✦ What type of questions will be on the exams—essay, multiple choice, fill-in?

✦ Are there past exams on file in the library?

✦ Will other work be required?

✦ When will the work be due?

✦ How will grades in the course be determined?

✦ What are the instructor's office hours? The location?

✦ Does the instructor have an outline of the most important terms and concepts to be covered?

✦ Does the instructor have a course website that supplements the classroom material?

These questions are a starting point. Others will occur as you go along. This is why having the phone number of another student in each of your classes can be very useful.

Many instructors provide a handout called a course syllabus. If you don't receive a handout, be sure to write everything down in your notebook. After class compare notes with other students.

Get Ready for the Paper Avalanche: The Smartest Way to Organize Your Notebooks

We suggest that you purchase a three ring notebook for each course. Select a different color notebook for each one. This helps avoid the "Oh no! I can't believe I brought the wrong notebook today!" experience. Be sure to write your name, address, and phone number in each notebook.

Purchase notebooks or inserts that have at least five color tabbed sections: the first contains the course syllabus and any other instructions specific to the course; the second holds paper for your class notes; the third holds assignments ready to hand in;

the fourth holds assignments/tests handed back; the fifth includes extra handouts from your instructor.

How do you place all the handouts into a three ring notebook? Either purchase a small, inexpensive hole puncher or find the location of a three hole puncher at a library or copy shop you can use.

Organizing your course materials in this way will make it much easier to be a successful student. Reminder: *After going to all this trouble, be sure to take your notebook and a pen to each class!*

Take Good Lecture Notes

Getting a good grade in a course starts with taking good lecture notes. The nature of human memory is such that people soon forget most of what they hear no matter how much they intend to remember.

Several days after a lecture, most students can recall only a small percentage of what the instructor said. If you ask a student who doesn't take notes to tell you about some details about what the instructor said last week, you will quickly see how important note taking is for accurate recall. So, unless you tape record the lectures or trade note taking with a classmate, you need to take notes at every lecture.

Always take notes in the same notebook. Date each day's notes. Always follow the last lecture with notes from the next lecture. Do not mix lecture notes from different courses and different days in the same notebook.

Lectures are like textbook chapters. Each usually has a main theme and makes several important points supported by examples and/or facts. If you listen for them, they will be easier to hear.

Since teachers don't necessarily teach in a way that makes a single note-taking system workable, it is wise to know more than one way of taking notes. Changing your note-taking method may help you to learn more like the instructor is teaching. For example, if the instructor is highly organized, the outline form for taking notes will work well.

─⋀─ You can read more about how to improve your listening skills by checking the Classroom Listening section of our website: AdultStudent.com

Outline Format:

Outlining is the most traditional way of taking notes. Outlines work well for lectures or talks where the instructor is organized and presents ideas in a logical order. Outlines begin with a main topic. Major points are given similar headings (A, B, C, etc.) followed by supporting points (1, 2, etc.). The advantage of using an outline form is that points can continue to be broken down into more minor points. There are two disadvantages to outlining. First, an outline can't be done if the speaker isn't organized. Second, students often get so involved writing that it is easy to miss part of the information.

Summary Method:

A second method of note-taking is the summary method. This method works particularly well for auditory learners. In this method you will listen for several minutes, and then write a short paragraph summarizing the main points. This method is particularly useful when an instructor uses long examples or stories, or is disorganized. The trick is to be able to write a couple of good sentences or a short paragraph without losing the next topic being discussed. This system doesn't work well if there are lots of facts you need to write down. Don't bother writing facts that are in your text or on a handout, though.

Mapping:

A third method of note-taking is called mapping. Mapping is a highly visual method and works well for visual learners. Mapping begins with a clean sheet of paper. Each main idea is placed near the center of the paper as it is presented. Once written, draw a circle around each main idea. (Most lectures won't contain more than three or four main ideas.) As significant details are given they are placed on a line that branches off from the circle. Minor details will branch from the significant details. The advantages to this method are that it is brief, flexible, and fits either organized or disorganized lectures.

⌁ See the AdultStudent.com website for Note-Taking Samples.

Are You an Active Learner?

It is important to learn how to take good notes because in college the responsibility for learning is the student's, not the teacher's. You cannot sit back passively and expect instructors to entertain you. It is not an instructor's responsibility to push you to learn or to make sure you get your assignments done. Succeeding in college is your responsibility, and that means being an *active* learner.

I got top grades. Mostly, it was because I attended all classes, and generally put a lot of time and effort into learning. However, I also made sure that every teacher knew my name by the end of the quarter. I always sat in the front of the room, and asked one or two intelligent questions during every class (the sort of question developed only by studying the class material outside of class). After I felt that the professor recognized me as a student that cared about the material covered, I met with the professor during his or her office hours and pursued some other aspect of the course material. In this way, I was able to get the professor to add a name to the face of the inquisitive and interested older student who sat in the front row. I'm sure that where my grade was borderline a couple of times, I was given the advantage because of the reputation I so carefully cultivated for myself. It couldn't have hurt. ~ MK

Good Study Habits Are Very Important

Your habits determine how much you learn during the time you spend studying. Two students may spend the same amount of time in classes and studying, but the student with good study habits learns more and gets a better education than the student with poor study habits. The chapters ahead will describe good study habits and show how you can develop them.

Enjoy Reading and Learning

Marion Drake, an instructor who works with adult students, says to buy a good dictionary and enjoy learning about the meanings of words. "We do best what we do most," she says, "so stop watching television. Spend lots of time reading." She says develop a passion for the subject and don't just memorize terms, learn what the concepts and principles mean.

Are Your Goals Self-Chosen?

Success is to reach a goal. Successful students are students who choose and reach their goals. It is less motivating and less satisfying to have goals that others have selected for you. Getting to any goal you select and work for makes you a successful person. The key is to make certain your goals are self-chosen.

⌁ See the AdultStudent.com website for an article on Developing and Setting Goals.

Action Review Checklist: College Success

◇ Do I act in ways that lead to success in my courses?

◇ Do I have well organized course notebooks?

◇ Do I take good lecture notes?

◇ Am I an active learner?

◇ Am I working to reach self-chosen goals?

Learning Team and Support Group Activities

1. This would be a good time to start a Learning Team with others in your specific classes. Exchange contact information. See if there is a group website that your team can use. Another way for online contact is to create a group list with your email software. This process is the same that many families and other groups use to send out information or messages. (See Chapter 2 for more hints)

2. You can create Learning Team groups for more than one class. Each would focus on the specific class but could also add more support like your personal support group.

How to Calculate Your Grade Point Average

You will probably learn about your grade in each course before the college sends you your grade report. If you don't want to wait, here is the method used for converting your course grades into the number called Grade Point Average:

A = 4 grade points for each course hour
B = 3 grade points for each course hour
C = 2 grade points for each course hour
D = 1 grade point for each course hour
F = no points

To calculate your GPA, list how many credit hours each course was worth and the grade for each course. Multiply the credit hours for each course by the grade's value. Then add up both columns and divide the grade points by the credit hours:

Course	Credit Hours	Grade	Grade Points
Psychology	3	C (2)	3 x 2 = 6
English	3	A (4)	3 x 4 = 12
Biology	4	B (3)	4 x 3 = 12
History	3	B (3)	3 x 3 = 9
	13 hours		grade points = 39

Grade Point Average = 39 ÷ 13 = 3.0

Each term you add the new total of all your college credit hours and divide that number by the total of all your college grade points. By the end of your second year, for example, what would your GPA be if you had taken 90 credit hours and earned 315 grade points?

Chapter 5

Online Learning

What is the difference between computer enhanced and online learning?

What are the advantages and disadvantages of online classes?

What does it means to "participate" in an online class environment?

How can you communicate effectively with your instructor and others in an online class?

What do I need to know to be successful if I decide to take a class online?

You have probably heard about classes that are being taught online since nearly all colleges are offering something online these days. One reason for the increase in classes offered online is that online classes fit a busy adult student's schedule. You enroll in online classes just like any other class, and the fees are the same as for a face-to-face class. There are differences though, and the frequently asked questions (FAQs) that follow should help you decide if online classes are for you.

1. *What sort of hardware, software or other equipment will I need?*
   Every school with an online program will have the basic hardware and software requirements listed. Usually, these requirements are listed right in the schedule of courses near where the online courses are listed. *Hardware* has to do with your computer itself, and *software* has to do with the kind of programs that you will need to access the school's online environment.

   Most schools do not require you to have the latest equipment, but some courses will have links to audio or visual elements. Some use CDs or DVDs that you purchase through the bookstore and use at different times during the course. If any of these newer media are part of the course, you will need to be able to access them at some point. It may be that you could use a school computer or a friend or family member's computer for a short-term session.

2. *I've only used a computer a few times. Won't I have a lot of trouble keeping up with everyone else?*
   Students taking online classes have varying computer skills when starting the class. Many schools offer an introduction to the class software with either an on-campus session or an online tutorial session. Usually, these sessions are at the start of the term and are free for the students. Most schools offer technical help both online and by phone, so you will have a real person available to help you with any problems. Some instructors are also willing to help with simple problems. Most students quickly learn valuable computer skills when taking online courses—a real bonus!

3. *I've heard of computer-enhanced classes. Are these the same as online classes?*

Computer-enhanced classes are still taught in a classroom, but the instructor will have supplementary material posted on his or her website. At a minimum, the course syllabus is posted along with other important class information and announcements. Some instructors will post articles and links that can help you study in greater depth and better understand the presented material. Other instructors may post exams on the website, or allow you to turn in papers electronically. The instructor will let you know what is available and how he or she will be using the site to enhance the classroom learning experience. Expect most of your classes to require some level of computer access.

4. *Won't I save time because I don't have to commute to and from school, and I won't have to sit in class for several hours?*

Sometimes students new to online courses think they will save a lot of time compared to what they would spend in a regular classroom. Oh, what a surprise when they find that online courses take just as much time as face-to-face classes. You might wonder why? There are several reasons:

✦ Although you don't have to commute to and from school, you will have to deal with general internet and computer problems. If you are already using a computer and accessing the web, then you know about the kinds of slowdowns that can occur. You also know that your own computer doesn't always behave the way you want it to. Another possible trouble spot is the school's server (the delivery system for their online courses). And then there is the school's software program that brings all the course components to the instructors and students.

✦ Your instructor will expect you to participate in the class through assignments and discussions. What this usually means is that you will write and post assignments to the class site. You will also be asked to carry out class discussions through asking and responding to questions from the instructor, yourself, and the other students. Naturally, the requirements for discussion will vary from course to course, but most instructors expect participation from every student. One way to think about discussions is that this part of an online course is similar to having discussions in a regular classroom with one big difference. In an online class, if you don't participate fully in discussions, it is the same as not going to class. *Online classes are not the same as correspondence courses.*

✦ The time it takes to type everything out is significantly longer than to speak your thoughts. This time difference has both a good and a bad side to it. The bad part is that it takes longer to do what you could do quickly in class. The good part is that comments made by students are usually more thoughtful and interesting. The simple act of putting your thoughts in writing slows down the shoot-from-the-hip sort of response that can come out when several people discuss a topic. Also, since everyone can read only one posting at a time, people can't interrupt the "speaker." Another advantage is that anyone can take the time to think over what he or she wants to say and the reader can take as much time as he or she wants to when reading. There is a written record of everything posted so it is easy to go back and reread postings at any time.

You can see that all of the above takes time. The advantage of online courses is that you can spend the time when and where you want. By this, we mean that you are able to do your work at any hour of the day (or night) and from anyplace you can access the school's site. Most instructors will give you at least several days notice before assignments are due or discussions are closed.

5. *How are tests given in online classes? Will I have to go to the school for tests?*
   Tests may or may not be given at a specific time and place. They may be given either online or at a test site. They may take any possible form from multiple-choice and true-false to take

home open-book tests. Often, online classes use essay exams for testing knowledge. Some classes even skip tests and require some sort of term project instead. Remember, the point of tests or projects is for you to demonstrate what you have learned in the class. You will want to look at Chapter 7 for more information about getting high grades on tests.

6. *What does the instructor expect from the students online?*
Your instructor will expect the same things from you in an online course as he or she would expect in a traditional classroom. Your presence will be all important, and your communication with your instructor is usually better than in regular classrooms. You will have much quicker access to your instructor through the course email, and likewise, your instructor can get messages to you that might take a week in a regular classroom.

7. *How can I express myself to both the instructor and the others in the class?*
The main means of online expression is through the written word. This means that how you say what you have to say is just as important as what you have to say. In online courses it is necessary to make sure that your words can't be misinterpreted by sounding sarcastic or critical. Some online environments use what are called "avatars," or comic-like graphical "people," to help you represent yourself and your emotions. Mostly, everyone writes in a sincere and thoughtful way, but it is worthwhile to monitor how you say what you want to say. For example, using ALL CAPS makes it appear you are shouting. Using "emoticons" such as :) for a smile or acronyms such as "lol" for "laugh out loud" helps indicate intent as well.

8. *What should I expect is reasonable for participation?*
We already mentioned that participation is a valuable part of an online class. Most instructors will tell you exactly what he or she expects of you in the way of participation. A fairly typical request is that you will be expected to post an original message (based on the instructor's guidelines) to the discussion area each week. In addition, you might be expected to respond

to the original postings of two other students during the same week. Often, though, there will be an ongoing discussion where you and others, including your instructor, will post more than two times. Each class will be different, each instructor will have different requirements, and the amount of participation will vary with the topic or the course. Sounds rather like any classroom, doesn't it?

9. *How do I find sources for papers if I'm not at the school library?* Every day there are increasing sources available by searching the internet. Many colleges and universities allow students to tap into their library databases from the web. You just need to use your student logon information. A better question to ask, however, would be about determining the credibility of the sources you find. For college papers, you need sources that will be accepted by your instructors. An article we've posted at the AdultStudent.com website gives many suggestions and tools to use when deciding the credibility of an internet source.

⌁ See AdultStudent.com for expanded resources on internet skills, online learning, distance education, emoticons, and authenticating resources.

◇◇

One of the reasons I enjoy teaching online is because of the unexpected fun things that happen or are said. About half way through one term a student announced with a "Wow! Online classes are like a classroom where everyone sits in the front row." He went on to say that, although a new experience for him, he didn't mind being in the front row because he liked hearing from more than the usual vocal few.

Another time, I was having lunch with Jeff, the chair of my department, at a nearby restaurant when a woman walked up to our table and started chatting with him. They talked about two or three things having to do with classes when Jeff asked if we knew each other. The woman nodded "yes" as I shook my head "no." Looking at my puzzled expression, she burst out laughing and told me that she was in my current class and had recognized me from the picture of me that I had posted in the class site. ~MK

◇◇

Action Review Checklist: Online Learning

◇ Do I know what computer hardware and software I need? Do I have a back-up option in place in case my computer doesn't meet the requirements?

◇ Do I understand the difference between fact-to-face classes and online classes?

◇ Do I know what the time commitment will be in an online class?

◇ Am I sufficiently motivated to keep myself on schedule so that I can fully participate in an online class?

Learning Team and Support Group Activities

You will need to adapt your support group activities to the online environment. You may want to set up a separate temporary group for each course.

1. Talk about the advantages and disadvantages of online classes and personal support groups. Do you have more or less contact with the group members than in face-to-face groups? How about with the instructor?

2. Discuss how to make online learning-team members feel included. How can you encourage each team member to participate fully in the group?

Chapter 6

The Best Way to Study

How do you create a study schedule?

How do you set study goals?

How can you get the most accomplished?

What is the most widely used and effective way to study?

How can you reduce your studying time?

What does a good study area consist of?

Do you use principles of psychology on yourself when you study?

Start By Listing Your Study Goals

Study goals help you focus your time and energy. They help you take the step-by-step actions that lead to reaching your dream for a better future. Setting goals is one of the best ways to motivate yourself to study efficiently and effectively.

Students who don't set goals or schedule their time are usually uncertain about what to do from hour to hour. Students who identify what they should study to pass a course and create a schedule to achieve their study goals, usually succeed more easily than they imagined. Here's how to set study goals and design a schedule to achieve them.

Determine What Your Study Goals Should Be

First, you have to ask, "What do I have to do to pass the course?" In most courses you have to do the following:

+ Attend class.
+ Participate in class discussions.
+ Pass quizzes.
+ Write papers.
+ Pass tests.
+ Complete projects.

To set up a study schedule ask these questions:

1. When is each test, paper, or project due?
2. How can I space my studying so that I don't put everything off until the end?
3. How much should I do each day if I wish to accomplish everything on schedule?

Answering these questions will allow you to design an effective schedule for reaching your study goals. You will know what to do and know when you can stop!

How to Manage Your Time

Fill in Your Calendar

Your greatest aid will be a calendar with spaces that you can fill in with important dates and obligations. Obtain a big year-at-a-glance calendar or a monthly calendar that you can tear apart and pin up on your wall. You want to be able to see at a glance what is ahead for the entire term or semester.

Fill in dates when examinations are scheduled and when papers and projects are due. Fill in all the times that you plan to do things with your family, meetings, concerts, and other events.

Create Weekly Schedules

Once you have a picture of your major commitments for weeks and months ahead, you can make up a weekly schedule of your classes, study hours, work hours and other obligations. A weekly schedule organizes what you do with your time. It shows you the places where you have extra hours you can use for studying. A schedule decreases the amount of time you waste.

When making your schedule:

- ✦ Budget some time to prepare for each class by reviewing notes and creating questions.
- ✦ Designate time for personal responsibilities.
- ✦ Reserve time to study course notes and write questions as soon as possible after each class.
- ✦ Study difficult subjects when you will have the least interruptions.
- ✦ Schedule time for your family and other important activities.

When you create a good time management/study schedule, it will motivate you. In fact, some students get so carried away we need to caution you to discipline yourself to stop studying! When you reach the scheduled time to stop, go get some exercise or do whatever you want to do. *Practice being a self-stopper!*

The problem for some students is that they study so much they use their time inefficiently. C. Northcoat Parkinson observed that "work expands to fill available time." You may have experienced this phenomenon. Let's say that you had in mind cleaning up the house or doing some yardwork during three hours available on Saturday morning. If you have three hours available, it will probably take you three hours to get the job done.

But let's say that before you start to work you learn that a very special person is coming by to visit and will arrive in about 30 minutes. You would probably be able to clean the house or mow the yard reasonably well in fewer than 30 minutes. What we suggest is that you decide what has to be done, do it, and then stop.

Time management experts often say that things not worth doing are not worth doing well. With less important jobs or matters don't waste precious time doing them as well as you can. Do them quickly, just good enough to get by. Use your precious time for more important things.

The main thing to accomplish is to control your activities rather than letting your activities control you!

A weekly time schedule that lets you fill in every half hour of the day, from early morning until late at night, will show you that you have many more hours each week than you might have ever realized. (Note: It will help your family if you post a copy where they can see it.)

Clocks and Success

See clocks as helpers, not oppressors. The better you learn effective time management skills, the more you can get done in the little time you have available.

Remember, you need clocks and a good personal organizer when your dream for your future is to succeed in college and still have a life. Clocks are your friends!

Make Daily "To Do" Lists

Take a few minutes each evening to list the important things that you have to do the next day. List those things most important to be done, then plan ahead. Here's what one student reported doing:

> On a daily scale, I prepare myself by getting my book bag ready to go out the door the night before. I make sure I have paper, pens, books, calculator—everything I will need for the next day's classes. This saves much searching time and also reduces stress the next morning. Along with all the supplies I *will* need, I make sure there is nothing in my bag that I *won't* need. This includes extra books, note pads, tennis shoes, a broken door handle—anything just along for the ride.

Your "to do" list gives you a way to make decisions about what you do during the day. It reminds you what is important to do and what to say "no" to. It also lets you know when you are done.

Get in the habit of putting your time and energy into your highest priority items. Don't deceive yourself by thinking that you will get to the really big project after you get all the little things out of the way. What happens is that by the time you finish the little, unimportant tasks your time is gone and you are too tired to work on the important project. The same student quoted above says:

> To me the most important thing is *putting first things first.* A set study time is a priority. Once time is decided upon, decide what needs to be done and *do it.* One way I can remind myself of the importance of my commitments is to picture the result of my actions. I ask myself "How will watching TV instead of studying affect my future?" This puts things in perspective and reminds me of my priorities.

Your Study Area

The environment where you study affects how well you learn. Here are some tips about what to do and not do:

Study in the same place at home and at school. Don't keep changing your studying locations. New places distract you.

Create a study area for yourself at home. Do what you can to make it the place where your attention is devoted entirely to your studying. If you study at a desk, keep it cleared off.

Use a comfortable chair. It will be a good investment to get a comfortable chair that adjusts for height and back support. Discomfort can lead to muscle strain and physical distractions.

Arrange good lighting. To reduce eye strain, your room should be well lit, with the main light source off to one side. A light directly behind or in front of you will be reflected from the glossy pages of your textbooks. A constant glare tires your eyes more quickly than indirect lighting. If you can't shift the lamp, shift your desk. Place the desk so that no portion of the bulb shines directly into your eyes.

I loved my study area. My kids kept giving me posters to hang on the wall, and soon I felt that my corner was like the typical student's study area. Over my desk was my favorite "hunk" poster of an actor standing on the beach wearing shorts. He and I spent a lot of hours together, and I can still visualize that poster. ~ MK

Neutralize Noisy Distractions

Use steady background sounds to neutralize distracting noises. Play your radio or stereo system *softly* while you study to create a steady background of "white noise" to mask occasional sounds. Experiment with stations, tapes, CDs, or streams until you find what works best for you. Instrumental (non-vocal) music is usually best.

➤ *NOTE:* Don't try to study with the television on.

If you want to watch a TV program, then watch it. But don't try to avoid feeling guilty about watching television by having your book open to read during commercials. Studying with the TV set on is *academic suicide.* Use television time as a reward after you have completed a study period, if you wish.

The Big Picture

Every person who is both busy and effective makes decisions about what to do and what not to do with their time:

✦ You started with your dream.
✦ You decided that going to college was the way to reach your dream of a better life.
✦ You confront your fears and concerns.
✦ You select courses that lead to what you want out of college.
✦ You imagine yourself succeeding in your courses.
✦ You identify what you have to do to pass each course.
✦ You develop monthly and weekly schedules for doing what it takes to complete course requirements.
✦ You make "to do" lists that help you focus on your highest priority activities each day.
✦ You stick with your daily schedule.

- ✦ You balance being a self-starter with being a self-stopper.
- ✦ You make a plan that leaves time for your family, your job, and other important activities.
- ✦ You become very good at learning, passing tests, and getting high grades.

What Psychologists Know About Learning

Psychologists have studied how people learn for almost 100 years. You can use their research findings to improve your ability to learn and remember. Their research also helps show what interferes with learning and remembering.

Here are some important principles to understand:

- ✦ The weakest form of learning is *passive recognition.* Studying is not the same as reading your Sunday newspaper. Reading your textbook is not the same as reading a novel.

- ✦ The strongest form of learning is *active recall.* This learning method is to read the material with curiosity, intending to remember what you read, and then from memory write or verbally give a summary of what you learned. Passively reading your textbooks and lecture notes over and over again is no fun and is an inefficient way to learn.

- ✦ How well you first learn and then later recall what you study is influenced by your study environment, study plan, and learning style.

The purpose of any test is to measure what you have learned. This means that to pass tests you must start by learning the information you will be tested on!

Textbooks are not written to entertain you. When it comes to studying, you must use study techniques that motivate you to mentally reach out and grasp important information.

Have You Had Trouble Learning?

Your past experiences in school may not have been positive. Perhaps you couldn't spell well. Maybe you reverse numbers and have trouble with phone numbers or your checkbook. You can understand if you are told instructions, but not if you read them. You may have had a learning disability and never knew it.

The Office of Disability or Counseling Office can help evaluate your difficulty and assist with tools to compensate. Everyone has strengths and weaknesses in learning. The trick is to accentuate your strengths and shore up your weaknesses. There's more on this in Chapter 9.

If you do in fact have a clinically diagnosed learning disability, the Americans with Disabilities Act along with Section 504 of the Rehabilitation Act mandate that persons attending schools receiving federal funding "not be excluded from the participation in, be denied the benefits of, or be subjected to discrimination under any program or activity." In other words, they must provide you with the assistance you need to develop your potential.

‑⋀‑ See AdultStudent.com for more resources on learning
   disabilities

The Secret to Rapid Learning and Success in Classes: Ask and Answer Questions

The most effective learning technique is very simple. It is to develop the habit of reading textbooks, taking lecture notes, and studying by asking and answering questions. When you do this you save many hours studying and have time to spend with your family, hold a job, take trips, attend concerts, and lead a balanced life.

Learning this study technique will take some effort because you will probably have to change some old reading habits. Such changes can be difficult. In the long run, however, the benefit is worth the effort, so stick with it.

How to Increase Your Studying Efficiency, Comprehension, and Ability to Remember

If you want to spend less time studying and remember better, focus on figuring out the important questions and the answers to them. The following steps will increase your learning speed, comprehension, and memory. Here is how to do it:

Skim Through Each Chapter Looking for Sources of Questions

You are sitting at your desk. The instructor has told you what chapters to study in the textbook. You open the textbook. Do you start reading the textbook as though it is a novel? No! Here is what to do:

First, look at the beginning of the chapter to see whether or not there are chapter objectives or a list of questions. Read them.

Second, look at the end of the chapter to see if there is a chapter summary. If so, read it right away! This is where you will find the important points the authors wish to stress.

> ➤ *NOTE:* When reading textbooks you save time by reading the chapter objectives and the summary at the end of the chapter before reading the chapter! (Quick activity: Do that now with this chapter.)

Third, skim through the chapter quickly. How do you skim a chapter? Glance through it rapidly the way you would look at a magazine that you are considering buying. You want a picture of the forest before you examine any trees. Look for titles, subtitles, illustrations, pictures, charts, highlighted words or phrases, and statements that will give you a basic idea of what the chapter is about.

Fourth, skim the chapter a second time turning titles, subtitles, and highlighted terms into questions. For instance, "Maslow's Hierarchy of Needs" is a section heading in a psychology textbook. When you see such a heading ask yourself "What is the hierarchy of needs that Maslow described?"

By asking questions about the material in the chapter, you alert yourself to the important points in the chapter. Reading in this manner is active rather than passive. When you ask questions, you will quickly develop a good sense of the questions the instructor will ask on tests.

What does a good question look like? It is generally not a yes and no question. It usually is fairly simple and starts with a phrase like:

Name three kinds of...

Describe the ways that...

List the important points about…
The pioneering research was done by…
The early research proved…
What does _____ mean?
The definition of _____ is…
The three stages of development are…

Read to Answer Questions

Now it is time to read. Read fairly rapidly. Read to find the answers to questions you asked while skimming the chapter.

> ➤ *NOTE:* In many instances, your questions and answers will be in titles, subtitles, or lead sentences and chapter summaries.

As you read, if you come to the answer to material that raises a new question, slow down, ask and then answer the new question.

Write a Summary

After you read the chapter to answer your questions, close the book. Write a short summary of what you have just read. You learn best when you immediately write a summary of the main points and facts from memory.

Recite What You Remember

If you commute in your own car or have a place where people will not be bothered by your talking out loud, a second way to learn course material rapidly is to verbalize what you have just read. Plan to take a few minutes skimming through the textbook before starting your commute. Then as you drive along, talk to yourself out loud about what you just learned.

The more sensory systems and muscles you involve in your learning the faster and more long lasting your learning will be. Talking to yourself shows you are study-smart!

Students who are not study-smart waste a lot of time by reading textbook chapters over and over without proving to themselves that they truly learned the contents of the chapter. They think, "I read it, I underlined it, I know what it's about." *Don't make that mistake!* Prove to yourself that you comprehend the chapter by answering questions out loud and writing chapter summaries.

> *NOTE:* Underlining or using a yellow highlighter will not lead to remembering nearly as well as writing or reciting what you know!

Make a List of Terms and Concepts

The fastest way to master a new subject is to focus on learning what the terms and concepts mean. To accomplish this quickly, make a list of words, terms, principles, and concepts that you will be expected to define, explain, describe, or understand.

Many students find that good old 3 x 5 (or 4 x 6) cards are useful. You write the term, concept, or principle on one side of the card. On the reverse side you write out the definition or explanation. Then, when it is time to recite and review what you know, you look at the card and try to state or write from memory the definition written on the other side.

Using the 3 x 5 cards is handy because you can carry them around with you instead of your textbook. Plus, they can be easily organized. A hole punch and a small card holder can be helpful. When you have a few minutes after lunch, on the bus, or while waiting for a class to start you can use the time to review concepts.

> *NOTE:* You do not need long blocks of time to study. You can study for a few minutes any time, any place!

Some commuting students make cassette tapes or use software to create audio MP3 files listing important terms and concepts. They use these recordings to give themselves an oral quiz as they drive or ride along.

Review Frequently

Frequent reviews help anchor your learning. With written summaries, audio files, and 3 x 5 cards you can go over what you've learned at any time. And, as you will see in the next chapter, you are well prepared to write practice questions.

The Benefits of Questioning

This study method is simple, saves time, and it works! You study for a limited time and then stop with a feeling of confidence that you know the material. You spend less time rereading chapters and doing other time-consuming study activities. This study method gives you the feeling that you've mastered the material. When you know you can answer questions correctly and make accurate summaries, you feel confident. Here is what one student wrote on an evaluation at the end of a course:

> When I read this chapter I thought "Oh, come on! It can't be that simple." But yes, Virginia, it is that simple. What a difference it has made! I was taking an economics course and getting nowhere... I started studying this way and was amazed at how much I retained. I've also found that the method of writing questions during lectures works well. It gives me a good idea of what is likely to show up on tests.

Some Difficulties With Skimming, Asking Questions, and Summarizing

Changing old reading habits is not easy. Especially if you are used to reading every word and trying not to miss anything. You have to use your mind actively when you ask questions and write summaries. While you are not reading for punctuation or grammar, "summary reading" takes more energy than passively reading printed pages. On the other hand, you learn so fast with this method you may feel that something is wrong because you are not having to study as much as you thought you would to get good grades!

Train the Way Athletes Do

This method is similar to the way athletes prepare for competition. Imagine yourself agreeing to run in a ten kilometer race several months from now. You will run with friends and it is important for all of you to do well. To be at your best, would you loaf around until the last few days and then prepare by running day and night until the time of the race? No. You'd start now with a weekly schedule of jogging and running. A little bit of practice on a regular basis prepares you the best. The same approach is true for effective studying and remembering.

When you use these study techniques you can expect the following results:

✦ The quality of your questions and answers will improve with practice.

- The amount of time it takes you to ask questions and write good summaries will decrease.
- You will be able to cover large amounts of material in far less time.
- You will find that you think up the same questions that your instructors ask.
- Your study periods will be shorter and you will feel comfortable stopping when your study goals have been reached.

Work With Your Concentration Span

Have you ever sat reading for awhile and then suddenly realized you didn't know what you just read? Discovered that your mind wasn't paying attention to what your eyes were reading? This is not an uncommon experience for students of any age.

The problem is that while you can make yourself sit and read hour after hour, your mind will take a break when it needs one. You are human. The length of time you can make your mind concentrate on a subject is limited even if you can make your body sit at a desk for hours.

Are you a morning person? Set the alarm for 5 AM and study before the rest of the household is up and leave chores for evening when your brain is disengaging. Does nap time after work help you feel mentally alert and full of "get up and go?" Or, can you get more done late into the night? If so, then go ahead and study until one or two in the morning. Select the time of day to study when your mental juices are most alert.

The way to make your study time more productive is to start with what you can do now and build on that. On the average, how long can you study before your mind slips off to something else? Twenty-five minutes? Ten minutes? Most students can concentrate on a textbook only 10 to 15 minutes before starting to daydream.

-\/- For more information on concentration see our website: AdultStudent.com

Record Your Study Time Segments

The next time you study, write down the time you start. Notice how long you read the textbook before your mind starts to daydream, then write down how many minutes you were able to concentrate. Don't set any particular goals for yourself yet. You first have to find out what is the normal span of time that you can concentrate reading textbook materials before your mind starts wandering.

Let's say that your study log shows that your average concentration span is about twelve minutes. This is the typical length for most beginning students. Even as low as five minutes, does not mean that you have an Attention Deficit Disorder. Accept ten to twelve minutes as your current level. Don't be bothered or upset thinking that you can't control your mind. Focus instead on increasing your concentration span in small, reasonable amounts.

Schedule Breaks and Take Them!
Set up a study schedule that fits your concentration span. Take a short stretch after each study segment and a long break about once an hour.

You will probably find the end of a study segment coming so quickly you will want to continue. *Don't continue without your break!* Keep your agreement with yourself. If you decide to take a stretch break after each short segment, then do so. *Do not allow yourself to study more than the allotted time.* Get up and stretch. Get a drink of water or step outside for a breath of fresh air or a hug from a loved one before starting the next study segment. The amount of self-confidence you develop from being in control of your mind and actions will probably surprise you.

Mix Study Subjects

Here are more principles of learning:

✦ When you learn one set of facts and then follow it with similar facts or material, the second set will interfere with your memory of the first and the first will interfere with your memory of the second.

✦ When you try to learn lots of information at one time you remember the first items and the last items best. The middle is most difficult to recall.

Charlene felt tired and discouraged. She studied hard for her three courses. She studied many hours evenings and weekends. No matter how hard she studied, however, she found it difficult to remember the material.

Did Charlene have a memory problem? No. Her problem was that she would study one subject all evening or all morning and then switch to another subject the next day.

The more you try to learn similar material at one time, the worse your recall will be. How can you avoid this problem when you have lots of material to study? The best way is to mix your study hours with dissimilar material.

> ➤ *NOTE:* Do not devote one long study period to one subject.

Switch subjects about once an hour. Always try to make your new subject as different as possible from the subject you have just finished. That way your mind can be assimilating one topic while you are reading about another.

Principles of Learning in Action

Here is an example of a study schedule using the principles described above:

15 min.—history
    1 min. stretch break
15 min.—history
    1 min. stretch break
15 min.—history
    10 min. break—drink some water, walk the dog
15 min.—math
    1 min. stretch break
15 min.—math
    1 min. stretch break

15 min.—math
    10 min. break—drink fruit juice, make short phone call
15 min.—English
    1 min. stretch break
15 min.—English
    1 min. stretch break
15 min.—English
All done! Reward—watch recording of *American Idol.*

Now that you know how to use the principles of learning to study efficiently and effectively, the next chapter will cover how to prepare for tests.

Action Review Checklist:
Create an Effective Study Plan

Use the following to rate how well you are doing at studying and following an effective learning plan:

◇ Do I have a calendar for the term marked with dates of all tests and assignments?

◇ Do I make weekly schedules of my classes and activities?

◇ Do I use daily "to do" lists?

◇ Can I do less important things quickly? Just good enough to get by?

◇ Do I set specific study goals for each course?

◇ Do I set up a schedule to achieve study goals?

◇ Do I follow my study goals schedule?

◇ Do I skim chapters first, ask questions, read the summaries, and then read to answer questions?

◇ Do I practice writing answers to questions and write chapter summaries?

◇ Do I make up lists of terms and concepts to use when I test my ability to recite definitions from memory?

◇ Have I created a good study area for myself?

◇ Do I study in short time periods and take breaks?

◇ Do I switch study subjects often?

◇ Do I stop studying when I said I would?

◇ Do I reward myself when I have successfully accomplished my study goals?

➤ *NOTE:* Revisit this checklist every three weeks to check your progress!

Learning Team and Support Group Activities

1. Talk about your ways of managing your time well. Discuss how it feels to do so many things by the clock.

3. Discuss what it feels like to be both a self-starter and a self-stopper. Share one thing that you complete at the "just get by" level yet feel fine about.

2. Talk with each other about your study habits. Find out what your study areas at home are like. Talk about how you handle distractions.

Chapter 7

How to Get
High Grades on Tests

What is the best way to prepare for exams?

How can you improve your chances of getting a difficult item right during a test?

Did you know that during an examination you can ask an instructor about test items?

What is an effective way to reduce test anxiety?

How to Get High Grades on Tests

An examination is a series of questions you must answer. This means that your grades are determined by your ability to answer questions, not by how much the instructor likes you.

To get a high grade on a test you must be able to answer the questions asked by your instructor. That is why we emphasize looking for possible exam questions every time you read your textbook or course notes.

Do you see how this works? If you want to get high grades on your exams, spend your study time writing examination questions based on your textbook, class notes, and reading assignments. Then you take these practice tests that you created, covering predictable test items. If you studied well, your test preparation work is over half-way done.

It is an inefficient use of your time to prepare for exams by reading, underlining, and rereading lecture notes and texts. No instructor conducts an exam by asking you to read your notes or textbook to him or her. Your instructors will ask you to answer questions based on *their* lecture notes, handouts, and the text-book. The point is obvious:

> ➤ To do well on tests, devote your study time to making and taking practice tests!

Make Practice Tests

Imagine that you are the instructor and have to write some questions that will test the class on the material covered. When you do this for each course you will be amazed at how close your test will match the one your instructor creates.

If you ever played an instrument in a concert or played on an athletic team you spent many hours rehearsing and practicing. Preparation for exams is the same. You prepare for exams by taking practice exams.

Write the Kind of Questions That Will Be On the Exam

What sorts of questions should you use? The same kind of questions your instructor will ask. Remember what we said earlier, successful students begin a course asking *when* tests will be given and *what kind* they will be.

Will the test be multiple-choice? True-false? Short or long essay? A combination of these? Write your practice tests using the same kinds of questions.

Practicing the same kind of test items you will be required to answer in a test situation helps you relax. It builds your confidence. You feel less tension about tests. You know you have studied the right questions, and you sleep better knowing you've studied correctly.

Other Sources of Exam Questions

Textbooks and *lecture notes* are your best sources of questions, but there are other sources as well. They include the following:

Old Exams

You can look at past exams without feeling guilty. It is not cheating to do this. Old exams show you what an instructor thinks is the most important information students should know. Some school libraries keep a backlog of old tests on file.

By looking at old exams you may find out:

1. Does the instructor repeat favorite questions every year?
2. Do test questions come primarily from lecture notes, the text, or from a variety of sources?
3. Does the instructor prefer multiple-choice, short-answer, true-false, or essay questions?

Student Manuals

The student manual written to accompany a textbook is an excellent source of exam questions. Student manuals contain true-false, multiple-choice, fill-in, and short essay questions. Even if your exam will be made up of questions that differ in style, the manual questions are still valuable.

> ➤ NOTE: There may be a student manual for your textbook
> *even if the instructor did not adopt it for the course.* Inquire
> about this either with the instructor, bookstore, or pub-

lisher. If a student manual exists, you can purchase it through the bookstore or directly from the publisher. It can be worth its weight in gold!

Other Students

Fellow students can be an excellent source of test questions. You can talk with students who have taken the course in past semesters to get information about the types of questions to expect. (Note: We're not suggesting that you ask someone who took the test earlier in the day for specifics about answers, just that they may know whether you can expect a bunch of fill-ins, multiple-choice, or short answers.)

Your Instructor:

Don't overlook asking your instructor for information about subjects and topics emphasized on the exam. As we said earlier, most instructors are happy to tell you what material they think is especially important. Some instructors will let you look at old tests. It won't hurt to ask questions such as:

- ✦ Will the test be objective, essay, or fill in the blank? Will it be a short, 20-item, true-false quiz? A 60-item multiple-choice test? A long essay test?
- ✦ How much time will be allotted?
- ✦ What proportion of the test will be based on lecture, readings, and the textbook?

Create a Folder with Practice Tests

Start each course with a plan. Read ahead in the textbook before class. This way topics your instructor discusses may not be entirely foreign to you. Take accurate lecture notes. Then as soon as possible, convert the information in your lecture notes and corresponding textbook chapters into questions.

Write your practice test questions on sheets of paper separate from your lecture notes, or use a spreadsheet or flashcard program. If you use 3 x 5 cards, place the question on one side and the answer on the other. The internet has several free and fee "flashcard" type software products available.

How to Quiz Yourself

1. Create a practice test from the questions you've been developing from textbook chapters, lecture notes, and other sources.
2. Take your practice test without referring to your books or notes. (Keep the answers hidden!)
3. If you are not sure of the answer to an item, try to guess. Make up answers as if you were in a real testing situation, trying to earn at least partial credit.
4. After you complete your practice test, check the accuracy of your answers.
5. Revise any test questions that need to be written differently.

This easy procedure lets you quiz yourself quickly. You look at your questions, give your answers, and then check to see if your answers were accurate.

Using your study time in this way creates a growing file of questions and answers that you are confident you could answer on an instructor's exam. When an exam is scheduled you don't have to pore over lecture notes and textbook chapters. Your folder of questions and answers or their stacks of question cards and quiz themselves. You could even show these to your instructor and get a view on how good your questions are.

Another way to take practice tests is to have a friend or family member quiz you. Later, when you feel ready, get together with your learning team or several classmates and quiz each other.

Do you have to drive a distance to get to the college? Here's how one student takes advantage of the time in her car:

> Besides doing 3 x 5 cards I record the questions on cassette tapes. I do a lot of driving. I play the tapes while I'm in the car. Hearing a question and saying the answer out loud helps. When I record the tapes I put on enough questions to make up about 15 minutes. Then I record about 15 minutes of music, changing back and forth between the two. For me the best music has a lively beat and no words: Bolero, Angel's Crossing etc.

Practice Tests Reduce Test Anxiety in All Subjects

Making and taking practice tests will eliminate the need for last minute cramming and greatly reduce exam panic. Short practice tests, taken every several days, will let you master small amounts of information each week.

This method helps reduce anxiety in math and science courses. Success in every course comes from frequent self-testing on the kinds of items that will be on instructor's exams. This method creates a feeling of familiarity and mastery even on math and science quizzes.

Before a mid-term or final exam, compile a comprehensive practice test made up of sample questions from your weekly tests. You'll be pleasantly surprised at how much easier it is to pass your final practice test when you have been taking weekly tests.

➤ *Remember:* To reduce test anxiety, keep taking practice tests!

The Advantages of Practice Tests

Predicting exam questions is the most useful technique you can use for learning the important concepts covered in your courses. As amazing as it may seem, students who write test questions and take weekly practice tests spend *less time studying and get better grades!*

You also remember what you learn much better than when you cram for exams. The research by psychologists shows that people remember material better when they review and rehearse it.

Some instructors will use test questions you write (and possibly give you extra credit for them)—especially well-written multiple choice or true-false items. It never hurts to ask the instructor if he or she would like to see questions you've written. Be sure to include chapter and page references, and mark the correct alternative. What a boost to sit down to a test and see your questions on it!~MK

The effectiveness of this study method has been proven over and over with thousands of students. This method helps you learn each subject quickly, get high grades, and obtain an excellent education. Your success in life is not determined by your course grades. It is a matter of what you know and what you can do. When you go to have your teeth cleaned do you ask the dental hygienist "What grades did you receive in school?" Probably not. You select professional services on the basis of what people know and can do.

How to Take Tests

General Guidelines

1. Read the instructions carefully. Glance at the entire exam to see where you'll earn the most points. Get a picture of how the test is laid out.

2. Look to see if answering questions that will be easy for you will earn as many points as the more difficult questions. If so, complete the easy questions first. After answering them you'll have more confidence, and you will be able to pass on to the more difficult questions. Do not start with the most difficult questions, get stuck on them, and then panic when you begin to run out of time.

3. Read each question carefully to grasp exactly what it is asking you to do. If the stem of the question says "What is an argument against…," then respond as requested. *Do exactly what the instructor requests!*

4. When you find an extremely difficult question or one you don't understand, move on to easier questions. Come back later to the ones you skipped. This reduces anxiety, saves time, and lets your subconscious mind search for the answer while you think about other items. Expect the answer to come to you just as you do when trying to recall a word or person's name. Skipping past hard items is also practical because sometimes you find a clue to the answer in questions that follow.

Three Kinds of Tests

There are three basic kinds of tests: tests that require you to *recognize* the right answer, tests that require you to *recall* the right answer from memory and write it down, and tests that require you to demonstrate *critical thinking* about the material you have been studying.

Recognition Tests

Multiple-choice, true-false, and matching items are tests of answer recognition.

> ➤ *Tip:* Many tests are given by using a scantron card for the answers. This makes grading the test easier but if you are in a hurry or under stress, it is easy to get on the wrong number for the answer. To avoid this problem use a ruler or the straight edge of another paper to line your marked answers and check your number every few answers.

Read recognition questions carefully, but answer them quickly. If the answer is not immediately obvious to you, put a mark by the item and come back to it later. Never leave a question unanswered, unless there is a penalty for guessing.

You may have heard an instructor or some expert say to never change answers on a test. That is not good advice. Research shows that a much larger number of students gain by changing answers than the number of students who lose points by changing answers. Be careful, of course, about changing answers, but your second thought, *if you have prepared well,* has a good chance of being correct. After the tests are handed back, check to see how many times answers you changed were right.

Multiple-Choice Questions. When you answer a multiple-choice question, eliminate the incorrect alternatives first. This saves time and increases your chance of determining the right answer.

Pay close attention to key words and phrases such as "*According to* Freud..." or "Which is *not*...."

Go through the test rapidly, answering questions you know you know. Next, go back to those that you skipped the first time. Before handing in your exam go back to see if you read each item correctly. Be alert to questions that say "always, never, or only." There are few absolutes in life or on tests.

Additional Multiple-Choice Test Taking Tips:
- ✦ Put your name on the answer sheet!
- ✦ Read directions carefully before answering anything.
- ✦ When requested to choose the "best" answer, read them all very carefully.
- ✦ Read all options before answering.
- ✦ When undecided, read each answer with the question.
- ✦ Watch for clues to complete the sentence in the correct grammar.
- ✦ If you really do not have a clue, choose the longest answer.
- ✦ The second and third choices are more often correct than first and last choices.

Matching Questions. Read the directions for matching questions very carefully. If the instructions say "Match those that are opposite from each other," you'll kick yourself later if you matched similar items.

Identify the easy matches first. This reduces the chance of errors on more difficult matches.

➤ *Tip:* Count the number of items in each column to see if they are equal. Cross off each item as you use it unless you may use it more than once.

True-False Questions. Don't waste time puzzling over true-false questions. They are usually the first items on a test with different kinds of recognition questions. Unfortunately, some students waste lots of time on several true-false questions. If an answer isn't obvious, move on to other questions. One or two true-false items aren't worth that many points. Besides, the answer may become apparent later in the test as you answer other items.

➤ *Tip:* True/False tests frequently have more true answers than false. Unless you are penalized for incorrect answers, guess. *Do not leave blanks.* You have a 50/50 chance of being right. Sometimes instructors will allow you to alter the wording of the statement to make it fit. Ask.

Recall Tests

There are three types of tests of recall: fill in items, short written answers, and long essay tests.

> ➤ *NOTE:* If an instructor says the test will be a *blue book* exam, you must go to the bookstore and purchase a thin book filled with lined pages that has a blue cover. It was designed specifically for essay examinations.

Fill-In Items. These types of questions are often drawn straight from the text you are currently studying. You will given a sentence with a word or phrase missing and be expected to "fill-in-the-blank" with the correct answer.

Short-Answer Tests. A short answer test given during a typical 50 minute class period may contain from 20 to 40 items. Such tests usually say to:

- ✦ Summarize the main findings of....
- ✦ Define the terms and concepts listed below.
- ✦ State the main criticisms against....
- ✦ Identify the parts in the picture:
- ✦ Briefly describe two arguments in favor of....
- ✦ List the factors leading up to....
- ✦ Name the basic steps to follow in....
- ✦ Explain why....

Your answers on short-answer tests will usually be phrases and incomplete sentences. You will not be asked to write long paragraphs so do not study that way. The instructor wants an easy to read list of phrases and brief statements.

> ➤ *Tip:* Before you start writing answers, write some of the information you memorized on the back of the exam.

Long Essay Questions. Take a little time to outline your essay before you start writing. When you have made sure you will cover the most important points you will be more confident and relaxed. Remember that the purpose of the essay is to demonstrate critical thinking about the material you've studied.

A well-written essay usually includes the following:

1. *Introduction.* Briefly describe the most important questions or present the main issues. Tell the reader what you are going to say and why.

2. *Use headings and subheadings.* Use headings for each major point or issue. Use subheadings every few paragraphs. Subheadings give the reader a quick understanding of the way you have organized your answer. (Notice how the headings and subheadings in this chapter show how the information is organized.)

3. *Demonstrate critical thinking.* "Critical thinking" does not mean to criticize! Critical thinking is your ability to comprehend, analyze, and evaluate conflicting views. This demonstrates a high level of mastery about a subject and is necessary to earn top grades.

4. *Give examples.* Illustrate your points with examples. They demonstrate that you really know what you are taking about.

5. *Provide definitions.* Show that you know what a term or concept means by giving its definition. Remember, the purpose of the test is for you to demonstrate depth of learning.

6. *Summarize.* Tell the reader what you have said. Be careful, however, not to include any new examples or information in the summary.

7. *Edit for clarity.* After you have finished writing, look through your essay to make certain you answered the important questions. Look for careless mistakes. Edit your answers and clarify your statements.

   ➤ *NOTE:* To get yourself started on an essay question, it can help to ask yourself what are the important social, historical, psychological, economic, or physical aspects of this question.

Critical Thinking Tests

Open Book / Take-Home Exams. Some instructors will give "open book" or "take-home" tests. An open book test is given in the classroom during the testing period. You will be allowed to use your text book and notes when answering questions. To score high on this kind of exam, you must interpret, analyze, synthesize, and evaluate course material in your answers.

Take-home exams work in much the same way as open book exams with the main difference being the amount of time you have to answer the questions. Often, you will be given the exam questions at one class period and will come back with your answers at the next class period. This means that if your class meets once a week you will have a week to work on your answers.

Exam Answers That Demonstrate Critical Thinking

Many students don't understand the difference between "C," "B," and "A" level work on their exams and papers. According to Benjamin Bloom, there are six levels of mental skills that demonstrate the kind of understanding a person has about a subject. Starting with the lowest level, knowledge, and building to the highest level, evaluation, students demonstrate depth of understanding of a topic or concept. Each level has key words that suggest the level of thinking. Levels one and two would probably receive a "C," levels three and four a "B." Five and six are "A" level work as long as other requirements for the assignment or test are met.

⎯∿⎯ Visit AdultStudent.com for more information on "Bloom's Taxonomy."

Sample of Critical Thinking in Graded Answers

As an example of the differences between the range of quality of a given answer, Cherie Costello provided the following example of a responses to an essay question from a test in a medical technician course.

Question: What is diabetes?

A "C" level answer is a short, memorized statement:
Diabetes is a disease in which the body has difficulty processing sugars, also known as glucose, or carbohydrate. It is caused by the inability of the pancreas to produce a substance called insulin. Insulin is responsible for converting glucose to glycogen which can then be utilized by the muscle and tissue cells, where it is united with oxygen to produce energy.

A "B" level response includes the above and adds information demonstrating comprehension and application of the knowledge:
When glucose cannot be converted to glycogen, it cannot be used by the body as fuel. If the body doesn't get enough fuel, cells will starve, resulting in hunger, weakness, and weight loss. The unprocessed glucose will build up in the blood, called hyperglycemia, to a level where it will begin to flow out in the urine, taking large amounts of water with it, thereby causing dehydration and increasing thirst. Excess glucose in tissues results in greater food available for bacteria, increasing the occurrence of infections. In addition, the body needs the metabolization of carbohydrates (glucose) in order to burn fats properly. Incomplete combustion of fats will cause the production of toxic acid substances called ketone bodies, which will result in a clinical condition know as acidosis or ketosis. In chronic diabetes there are changes in the small blood vessels throughout the body, such as thickenings and lesions, the most serious in the retina and kidneys. Problems with vision and blindness, kidney damage, and peripheral neuropathy caused by these vascular changes are common. With decreased fat and carbohydrate combustion, the brain will starve, leading to eventual coma and death.

And finally, an "A" level answer begins with the above basic information, but in addition includes analysis, synthesis, and evaluation:
Though diabetes is generally considered a metabolic disorder characterized by hyperglycemia, the actual cause may be any of a number of problems. The lack of insulin can be due to:

1. Lack of synthesis of insulin by the islets of Langerhans cells in the pancreas.
2. Synthesis of an abnormal insulin molecule.
3. Failure of the pancreas to secrete the synthesized molecule. Resistance to insulin due to...
4. Defects in insulin receptors in the liver where the glucose is converted to glycogen.
5. Anti-insulin antibodies formed by the immune system.
6. Accelerated rate of insulin breakdown. Treatment of the disease syndrome must rely on proper diagnosis of the underlying cause.

Initially blood sugar levels may be controlled entirely by diet, but many will develop the need for exogenous insulin treatment at some point. Complications, such as peripheral vascular insufficiency may result in loss of a limb due to persistent infection. Loss of vision, gallstone formation, and acceleration of atherosclerosis predisposing myocardial infarct are all possible complications of the disease process and contribute to a compromised quality of life for the diabetic patient. Well controlled diabetes management has reduced considerably the possibility of death from diabetic coma, but the complications from kidney damage, infection, and arteriosclerosis are often the deciding factor in the lifespan of the afflicted patient.

When Questions Puzzle You

What can you do with a question that stumps you? Skip it until the end of the test. While answering other items, you will probably recall some information related to the answer. Before turning in your exam write down *anything* that demonstrates some learning. Do not leave an answer blank. It gives an instructor a negative impression. If you can't figure out the exact answer, you can probably come close, and you might get partial credit!

Nervous? Write Comments About the Test

If your heart is pounding, your palms sweating, and you start to feel overwhelmed, imagine the following statement at the top of the test: "Feel free to write comments about the test items."

Research by psychologist Wilbert J. McKeachie, an expert on teaching and learning, discovered that students who received examinations with the "Feel free to write comments..." statement printed at the top of tests, did better on the test. He found that it did not matter if students actually wrote anything about the test or not! The mere presence of the statement improved the scores of many students. This means that if you feel anxious or nervous or have fears of failing, it will help to write comments in the side or back of the test.

You Can Ask Questions During the Exam

Exam questions are not always clear. Instructors know that. Many times they create exam questions in a hurry late at night and sometimes a question is not worded well. That is why many instructors will talk with you about a test question during the exam.

If, even though you studied well, there is still a question you don't understand, go up to the instructor and ask about it. Say "I don't remember this material from the lecture or the text. Where was this information presented?" Or, "there are several correct answers to this item, which one do you want?"

You have nothing to lose by asking for some hints. The instructor will not give you the answer, but may remind you where the information was located in the textbook, or such, which could trigger your memory.

What You Gain From These Test-Taking Methods

Students who use the methods described in this chapter:
+ usually receive high grades on tests.
+ earn more points for answers than predicted.
+ feel confident and relaxed during tests.
+ complete exams in time available.
+ seldom misread the test questions or answer questions incorrectly.
+ do not waste time on questions that stump them.
+ do not put wrong or irrelevant information in answers.
+ get more points on written items that let them "pad" their answers for other parts of the test.
+ seldom develop exam panic.

+ get higher grades in their courses.
+ demonstrate to the instructor that they have mastered the course content.
+ sleep well the night before the exam!

Action Review Checklist:
Success in Preparing for and Taking Tests

◇ At the start of each course do I find out what kind of examination the instructor will use?

◇ After each class do I write and then quiz myself on possible test questions?

◇ Do I practice taking the tests I create every week?

◇ When I take tests, do I use the methods recommended in this chapter?

Learning Team and Support Group Activities

1. Talk with each other about the kind of test you will be taking. Is it multiple choice, true/false, short answer, essay, etc.? Find out how others study for specific kinds of tests. What is similar or different about how each person prepares?

2. Discuss which material being covered in the test is the most difficult for each of you. Get tips from each other about how they deal with difficult material.

3. Look at Bloom's Taxonomy at the website and discuss the different levels of thinking he describes. Talk about how you could demonstrate higher levels of critical thinking in your term papers. What are your opinions about the "A," "B," and "C" levels of critical thinking in your term papers as well as on exams?

Chapter 8

How to Write Excellent Papers

What does asking questions have to do with writing your papers?

What should the starting point of your papers be?

Did you know the ability to write excellent papers may depend on how well you know how to use the library and find resources?

How can I avoid plagiarizing?

What is the difference between a barely acceptable paper and an excellent one?

The Secret to Writing "A" Papers

You do not have to have a high IQ to write a term paper that gets an "A." All you have to do is:

+ always keep in mind you are writing your paper for one person, your instructor.
+ select a topic interesting for you and one that your instructor feels is important.
+ show your instructor your outline for your paper before putting a lot of work into it.
+ make your paper a series of answers to important questions.
+ demonstrate your critical thinking skills.

Interview Your Instructor

Select two potential topics for your paper. A good way to investigate a research topic is to consult an encyclopedia. *The Encyclopedia Britannica* (print, CD, and online) is an excellent resource. If it covers a subject, it will provide you with a comprehensive summary and the important viewpoints about it. An internet search at a site such as wikipedia.org can also provide resources, but you need to be careful about what you choose.

-\/- Please check AdultStudent.com for guidelines on authenticating and evaluating online resources.

Make a list of important questions and issues for each topic. Work up a one page outline of what you would do with each topic.

Meet with your instructor before you start writing your paper. Interview the instructor to find out which topic the instructor feels would be better for you to write about. Ask the instructor if there are important references you should look at and refer to in the paper. Ask the instructor "What important questions and critical issues should I cover in the paper?" Listen well. The instructor will probably tell you exactly what he or she will want to see in the paper. You make things much easier for yourself when you do this!

Start With Questions

Begin your research by listing specific questions you intend to answer in your paper. If you aren't certain how to start, go to the library and talk to one of the reference librarians. They can help you find sources of information you don't know about. That is what their job is. Use their expertise.

The Computer Can Do Your Search

Once you have a list of questions, start looking for answers. Go to your library and ask a reference librarian. Also, many college libraries have courses that teach you how to search for periodical information and write a research paper. In most, your search for information sources will start with a computer terminal and online content providers such as EBSCO or ProQuest. When using periodical databases, it is now possible to email the article or abstract (summary) to any email address you choose. The abstracts of articles are a quick way to research relevant data. You no longer have to print articles you want to look at further. You can just send them to yourself. In addition, many institutions allow students to log on to these sources from home, laptop, or mobile device.

Card catalogs are also now online. The online computer system tracks availability of books and journals and even allows you to reserve materials that are in other locations or at other libraries. If you are unsure of how to search or navigate the catalog, ask a librarian for help.

In your search, you can access information by author, subject, title, and more. You'll probably want to start with the subject index and search using some keywords that you've already identified in your question development.

Use your imagination when searching the subject index. Look under every topic you can think of. As you find sources, scan them for other aspects you hadn't thought of and look there. Make notes of book titles and authors, and always write down the complete call number of the book. The *call number* is the library's code number that tells you exactly where the book is shelved.

> ➤ *NOTE:* When you see the statement "reserve" or "reserve desk" by a book, you will *not* find the book in the open shelves. An instructor has had the book placed in a special reserve section where it can be signed out for a limited amount of time—usually several hours to overnight.

Periodical Sources at the Library

The most recent information on a subject appears in professional journals long before it is written up in books. Search your library's online catalog for keywords related to subjects of interest.

Be sure to look under "Journal," "American," and "National" in any alphabetical listings. The journals of professional groups are often titled *The Journal of...*, *The American...*, or *National Society of...*, etc.

When you write down call numbers for books and journals, you will notice that the books and journals with information about your topic will be located in two or three places in the library. When you go to these locations in the stacks, you will discover other useful books and journals nearby.

From the journal articles you learn about books to research. From the books you will learn about journals that focus on your topic most frequently.

Skim articles and books first to get a general orientation. When you find useful data or passages you may want to quote in your paper, record the name and date of the publication, the title of the article or chapter, and page numbers, and write down or photocopy the quote exactly as it was printed. It is very frustrating when you can't remember which author you quoted or which statement in your notes is your own summary. Libraries have photocopiers and often scanners available. You will save time using them.

The old standby, *The Reader's Guide to Periodical Literature,* has by and large been replaced by the online databases which generally are able to find most of the current consumer articles. Don't discount consumer magazines as a source of information, because some scientific research is published directly in them. Besides, the information is less technical than in professional journals and books. The *Readers Guide* is still helpful for finding older articles.

If you do not find the information you need in your library, your librarian can search local, national and even international sources to obtain the most up-to-date references for you.

> *NOTE:* Libraries have greatly expanded their video and audio selections. If you find you learn easier by watching or listening, consider using these convenient resources.

While the library is still a (mostly) quiet place filled with books and journals, the rules have changed somewhat. In addition to free wireless connections and the availability of the latest multi-media items, you can generally eat and drink in sections of today's libraries—perfect for that extended research session. The one thing that has not changed is that the librarian is a very helpful person.

Search for Answers

You'll discover that by having questions in mind that you want to answer, you can quickly cut through the massive amount of material that could otherwise distract you. By reading to answer your questions, you avoid the needless loss of hours wondering how much you should include in your paper.

Expect New Questions

In the process of answering questions, new questions will most likely arise. You may find that as you do your research you need to change the original questions in some way or add some new ones.

Write a Rough Draft

Now that you've gathered your information, it is time to write a rough draft about your questions and the answers you found. Write your first draft quickly. Don't waste time trying to make your first draft your final draft.

Start by presenting your questions and explaining why they are important.

Write the answers to each question. Make your point and back it up with examples and sources. Answers to questions are more believable when they are clear and well supported.

Quote from your sources. Brief quotes, paraphrases, facts, and figures have more effect than personal impressions, opinions, or generalizations. Give exact references for your quotes, paraphrases and facts.

Arrange your answers so that they connect in a logical way. Connect them by saying, showing, explaining, or demonstrating how they are related to each other. They may be ordered chronologically, topically, or procedurally, for example.

Demonstrate Critical Thinking

Instructors don't want you to parrot back what some authority has said. They want you to show that you can think intelligently about the subject and demonstrate critical thinking.

To show critical thinking, review the elements of critical thinking covered in the previous chapter. In your discussion show how well you comprehend the principles and perspectives. Don't pick one viewpoint and present it as right while others are wrong. Analyze the strengths and weaknesses of one perspective and the strengths and weaknesses of a contrasting perspective. Evaluate and synthesize the perspectives.

Your life experience gives you an advantage over younger students here. You know there are always two sides to a story (at least). Present both sides plus your own ideas about what the material means.

Summarize and Draw Conclusions

At the end of your paper summarize the main points and add two or three conclusions. The summary explains what you have done in your paper, justifies your conclusions, and demonstrates critical thinking. Be sure to check your summary against the introduction to your paper. Do they match? If not, revise your introduction.

Listen to Your Paper

The best way to quickly determine if your paper makes sense is to read it out loud. When you read it aloud, a rough sentence structure or a statement that does not make sense will be very apparent. After reading your paper aloud to yourself, consider reading it aloud to a learning team member or classmate.

Correct Your Grammar and Spelling

Make sure that your spelling and grammar are accurate. Use a spell checker or a dictionary when in doubt. Have someone else proofread your paper. Few things bother instructors more than poor spelling and bad grammar. Instructors tend to give higher grades to papers clearly typed, grammatically correct, and free of spelling errors.

Consult Your Instructor

Make an appointment to go over your first draft with your instructor. Many instructors will give you good feedback about any necessary revising you will need to do if you want an "A."

Revise and Rewrite

The real writing of any paper, of course, takes place when you rewrite and edit your first draft. Most good papers require several revisions before achieving the final version.

During your rewriting, revising, and editing ask yourself:

+ Have I clearly stated the questions my paper will answer?
+ Are the questions I selected important to the topic and cover it well?
+ Have I answered the questions effectively?
+ Is my writing interesting to listen to?
+ Have I corrected grammatical, punctuation, and spelling errors?
+ Does my summary accurately cover the main points of my paper?
+ Do my conclusions demonstrate critical thinking and cover what I learned in the process of writing the paper?

> *NOTE:* If you feel the need for help with your writing, contact the English department. English departments usually run a writing skills center for non-English majors. It is worth looking into.

Caution: Do Not Cheat or Plagiarize

According to a poll of 1000 college students conducted by *US News & World Report,* 84% said they believe they need to cheat to get ahead. Most of the cheating is to copy homework or purchase term papers from websites. Some students cheat on exams with PDAs or text messages.

Some students see nothing wrong with copying passages from a book or magazine article and turning in the paper as his or her own work. They rationalize their actions as having too much pressure to do too much work and feeling that their career opportunities require them to get high grades by any means that they can.

Trying to pass off someone else's work as your own is called *plagiarism*. It is a form of lying. There are many negative consequences to plagiarism. You can be flunked if you are caught. But even if you succeed, *you subvert your self-confidence when you face real-life career challenges!* Plagiarism also diminishes your opinion of your instructors if they allow you to get away with it.

Colleges are taking steps, by-the-way, to deal with the problem of plagiarized term papers. The website *www.plagiarism.org* has more information and supplies instructors with a high-powered program that can detect plagiarism in a paper.

It is human to consider taking shortcuts, but plagiarizing is not worth the risk. Plagiarism is unethical and usually illegal.

It really is quite simple to avoid plagiarizing: *cite your sources.* You can use quote after quote in your paper, as long as you define them as such and provide the source of each quote either in context or in the notes. Mind you, your grade may be affected by using too many quotes and showing too few critical thinking skills.

> ➤ *NOTE:* It is plagiarism to turn in a paper written by another student. This means you don't let another student copy your work, you don't copy theirs, and you don't do their work for them.

Make Your Papers Look Good

If you want a top grade, produce a clean, sharp looking paper. Type or print out all your papers. Instructors prefer printed, easy-to-read papers because of their constant struggle to avoid eye strain. If you don't have keyboard skills, consider taking a typing class. It is one of the best self-improvement efforts you can make and will save you lots of time in the years ahead. (Many English departments have their composition courses conducted as computer labs, so you might want to take an English composition course. It is also a good way to develop computer literacy if you are not familiar with computers.)

Make your paper as professional looking as possible. Use clean white paper. Double space the lines. Keep handwritten corrections on the final copy at a minimum.

Be sure to follow all directions your instructor gives for the way you should do footnotes, references, and other procedures. It is a waste of time and energy to devote hours to a paper only to have it returned as incomplete. *The consequences of failing to follow directions can be costly.*

A word to the wise: Hand in a paper you are proud of! If it were a business report that would affect your chances for a pay increase, would you submit it the same way?

> ➤ *NOTE: Always* make a copy of your paper. The original could get damaged or lost. Play it safe. Keep a copy and be sure it is saved on a second computer or flash drive.

Action Review Checklist: Success in Writing Papers and Using the Library

◇ Do I write papers using the question and answer format?

◇ Have I asked the reference librarian for suggestions about where to look for information?

◇ Do I use the card catalog, microfiche, or online system to track down good reference sources?

◇ Do I get up-to-date information from professional journals?

◇ Are my quotes and references accurate?

◇ When my first draft is completed, do I ask the instructor to look it over and give me suggestions for improvement?

◇ Do I check for correct grammar and spelling?

◇ Do my papers reflect my ability for critical thinking?

◇ Am I proud of what I hand in?

Learning Team and Support Group Activities

1. Find out if everyone in your learning team knows how to use your college library. What tips can you give each other about efficient use of the library resources? Is everyone familiar with online library resource material?

2. When you are developing ideas for papers, bounce topic ideas and key questions back and forth. Choose topics that interest you. It helps to feel enthusiastic about your topic. After you have chosen your topic, revisit the information in Chapter 7 about critical thinking. Discuss how you can help each other in writing papers.

REVIEW AND PREVIEW

The first eight chapters of this book covered basic information on how to get started in college, how to succeed in your courses, and how to meet online requirements. By now you have learned that your college provides helpful services and assistance on each of the areas covered in the first seven chapters. If you find yourself struggling with any of these challenges go talk to someone in the college counseling department. The people there are friendly and very good at problem solving student difficulties. They will help you stick with your education plan.

The previous chapters covered important academic skills, the rest of the book covers non-academic challenges. Without good life skills, you reduce your chances of getting the education you desire and the career you seek.

In some classes, for example, you will be required to team up with a few other students to do a project. Part of your grade will be based on how well your team does. As a member of a learning team, like with a work place team, you must deal with differences in personalities, working styles, and cultural backgrounds. In the next section you will find guidelines for understanding and successfully resolving predictable conflicts with others.

Do you handle pressure and constant change well? Select and transition into a new career easily? Enjoy working for an employer that does not provide job descriptions? Are you flexible and resilient? The next chapters show how to be resilient and thrive in a world of non-stop change.

Chapter 9

Learning Styles and Teaching Styles: How to Influence Instructors

What is your preferred learning style?

How do difficulties in a course stem from a conflict between a student's learning style and the instructor's teaching style?

What is a college instructor's minimum qualification?

How can I improve the teaching I get?

What can I do to overcome a poor start in a course and get a good final grade?

Learning Styles: They Can Help or Hinder

The first day of classes can be overwhelming. Each instructor passes out the course plan (called a "syllabus") with due dates for readings, papers, exams, and projects. The instructor will explain how the class will proceed along with expectations for success in the class. You may leave class wondering how you will be able to manage all the assignments for all your classes.

Things tend to settle down during the second week. But what if you discover that you have an instructor who teaches in a way that makes learning difficult for you? A reality of college is that no matter how good of a student you are, you will take courses from instructors who don't teach the way you learn. Research into why some students do well with one instructor but not another, uncovered a simple truth about academic life:

The way an instructor teaches will not fit with the way some students learn.

Instructors don't deliberately try to make life difficult for you, but it helps to remember that most instructors teach using the style that reflects the way they learn best. If you want clear guidelines from an instructor, but take a course from someone who provides little direction, you may flounder. If you prefer classes where the instructor encourages discussion and encourages students to develop their own views and answers, then you may have trouble in a straight lecture class.

Research findings and experience have identified the following important differences in how people learn.

Visual vs. Auditory vs. Tactile Learning Styles

Have you ever noticed that you can tell a person something but it doesn't register unless you write it down for them? Or that someone might read a note you've left, but the message didn't get through to their brain? That is because people differ in how information gets into their consciousness.

Some people learn best by reading. They must see something in writing before they believe it and remember it. Other people learn best by listening. Information doesn't stick well unless they hear it. Then there are those who need hands-on experience in order to understand. What is your natural style?

- ✦ Do you prefer to listen to the radio or read newspapers for the news?
- ✦ Do you remember what you read the best or what is said to you?
- ✦ Would you rather read what an expert has written on a subject or hear the expert talk?
- ✦ Are you a person who would rather be shown or read step-by-step instructions, sometimes several times, before trying it for yourself?

Based on your answers to these questions, which learning style do you tend to prefer? Auditory, visual, or tactile?

Everyone learns by each way, of course. A learning style is not an all-or-nothing situation. Yet the differences between people are sometimes extreme enough to cause problems.

Visual Learning Style

If you learn best visually, you may be in trouble with an instructor who emphasizes class discussion, doesn't use handouts, and doesn't write much on the board. *The solution with a verbally oriented instructor is to:*

1. Take good notes on what the instructor and your classmates say. After class fill in sentences and compare notes with other students.

2. Ask the instructor for suggested articles or books that will let you read the information you need to understand better.

3. Consciously work at listening and remembering what the instructor says. *TIP:* One woman wrote to us saying that she types her lecture notes immediately after every class. Many students today take laptops to class to record lecture notes.

4. If you are confused about a point, ask the instructor to tell you again and write down what you hear.

5. Ask your instructor if an outline of the lecture is available.

Auditory Learning Style

If you have an auditory style, you may have difficulty with a visually oriented instructor who hands out written assignments without discussing them. This instructor may assign textbook material and outside readings that are never discussed. *The solution with a visually oriented instructor is to:*

1. Find classmates who will tell you what they learned from the textbook readings. (In turn, you can help them with their lecture notes.)

2. Ask permission to record your classes. As you listen to the recordings later, add important information to the notes you took in class.

3. Dictate the main points from the reading assignments and handouts onto cassette tape, your computer, MP3 recorder, or digital memo device and then listen to them while doing other things.

4. Consciously work at improving your ability to acquire information visually. (*Note:* For professional help, go to the reading improvement center or the campus office of disabilities.)

Tactile Learning Style

If you are mainly a tactile learner, then you will have to be creative in how to turn lecture classes into meaningful information. *The solution with either a visually oriented or a verbally oriented instructor is:*

1. Take notes, then rewrite your notes soon after class. You might try rewriting notes several times until you "get it." Also, you might experiment with a different system of taking notes. (Review Chapter 4.)

2. Visuals will be especially important to you. You should try to get copies of your instructor's visuals and even notes.

3. Be sure to copy all whiteboard information from each class.

4. Find out if there are any exercises or outside experiments that you could try that could help with your understand of the material. Perhaps there is a lab available.

5. Find out if the class is "computer enhanced," Some instructors post useful supplemental material on the course site.

6. Try to teach the information to someone else. Teaching another often helps you understand more about what you are teaching.

Learning Style Inventory

Educator David Kolb created the Learning Style Inventory based on four ways that humans learn. Most of us use a combination of styles, but we each seem to have a preference for how we learn. Kolb identified four main approaches to learning: concrete experience, abstract conceptualization, active experimentation and reflective observation.

What does this mean to you, the learner?

People who favor *concrete experience* learn best when interacting with others in a classroom. Open class discussion, exercises, and small group projects are favorite ways of learning. If this describes you, then you are more of an auditory learner.

Those who fall mainly into the *abstract conceptualization* category tend to like facts and figures and would rather have an instructor who mainly lectures and supports lectures with visuals like handouts, PowerPoint presentations, and text readings. Even though lectures require listening, the handouts and other visual prompts help this primarily visual learner to understand the material presented.

Active experimenters like doing things. People who favor this learning style, like concrete experience learners, prefer small group discussions and projects. In addition, they also tend to like homework assignments. If you are an active experimentation learner the main difference between you and the concrete experience person is that you are happy working alone while the concrete experience person likes working with others. Active experimenters use more of an auditory style when learning.

Reflective observation learners prefer lectures and like to think about information from an impartial perspective. These auditory and visual people take time to observe before making judgments, and often consult multiple sources for information. If this is your main learning style you may have difficulty with an instructor who believes that telling students what they should know is a sufficient way to teach. Your need for more information might lead you to probe deeper into a topic on your own, sometimes to the dismay of the instructor.

Another issue to be aware of as a reflective observer is that you may be ready with questions and observations about the last discussion when the class meets the next time. Often, however, the class has moved on and you will not be given a chance to ask your questions. (This would be a good time to schedule a meeting with your instructor.)

Learn to Appreciate Human Differences

We humans are all born with different temperaments and different ways of functioning in life. That is simply the way things work. When you experience conflicts with instructors or classmates at school, at work, or in your family, question your attitudes about others. If you experience an irritating difference, use that as an opportunity to learn more about human nature. You might as well, because you won't change other people by complaining and criticizing them!

The better you know yourself, the more skillfully you will manage your learning style and the easier it will be to succeed in college!

‑⋁‑ Please check AdultStudent.com for more information on how temperament can affect your group dynamics.

Coping With Poor Teaching

You've had enough experience to know that every occupation has a few people who are excellent, many who are competent, and some who are poor at their craft. Don't be surprised when you discover that the same principle is true of college instructors. You will have a few who are outstanding, many who are very good, and a few who make you wonder how they keep their jobs.

A fact of college life is that college instructors can hold teaching positions without ever taking classes on how to teach. They do not have to be certified to teach, as do elementary and high school teachers. At the college level the responsibility for learning is on the student, not on the teacher. College students are expected to learn what the course covers, no matter how deficient in teaching skills the instructor is.

Seven hundred students at the University of Wisconsin were asked to list what annoyed them most about their professors' ways of teaching. The ratings were collected anonymously and covered all courses in all subjects. The complaints listed by the Wisconsin students were similar to student complaints at many colleges:

✦ Poor course organization poor planning, important material rushed at the end.

✦ Too many videos shown, often selected at the last minute.

✦ Poor teaching mechanics: use overhead transparencies or presentations with tiny print, speak too fast for students to take notes, too much writing on the board, standing in front of the board.

✦ Poor testing and examination procedures, unfair or confusing grading.

✦ Negative mannerisms: distracting gestures and facial movements, inappropriate attire.

✦ Poor speaking skills: monotone voice, speak too fast or too softly, bad grammar, ramble, swear, get sidetracked on irrelevant topics.

✦ Disrespectful of class time: come in late and stop early.

✦ Don't want to be interrupted with student questions, talk down to students, sarcasm, act superior.

Practical Suggestions

What do you do when a teacher is less than ideal? Do you get distressed? Complain? Not study or put effort into the course?

By now we hope you have realized that finding a really good match between yourself and an instructor does not happen all the time. As an alternative to feeling like a victim and blaming the instructor for your poor grade, we have the following suggestions:

1. Before registration ask around to find out about various instructors. If you have a choice between instructors, you'll know which one to choose.

2. Try to get as much out of every course as you can, regardless of who your instructor is or how much the teaching style does not fit your preferred learning style. Be open to trying a new way of learning.

3. When you have a difficulty understanding what is happening in a course, make an appointment to talk with the instructor. Be prepared to ask for what you want.

4. If you still have problems, go to the office or center that teaches studying and reading skills. The specialists there can be very helpful.

How to Influence Your Instructors

Give Feedback to Instructors

You can influence how your instructors teach. When an instructor does something you appreciate, let them know right away. Don't wait until you fill out the course evaluation at the end of the course. After class, compliment them or hand them a note. When you and the other students praise good teaching, you'll get more of what you like and less of what you don't like.

If you want to tell an instructor that there is something that needs to be improved, give a specific example of what you don't like and what you would like instead.

How to Turn a Bad Situation Around

So here you are, you totally blew the midterm, got a "D" on your project, and could end up with a "D" or "F" in the course. Is your situation hopeless? Not at all. You can often salvage a bad grade.

First, write about your feelings or talk to a friend about how you feel. Students who express their feelings when they are disappointed or upset bounce-back better and are more resilient than students who don't express their feelings.

Second, do not take a low score personally! Your grade is feedback on how well you demonstrated your knowledge about the subject to the instructor in the way the instructor wanted. It is not a grade about you as a person. Almost every instructor has a story about a student who protests "But I thought you liked me! Why did you give me a low grade?" A test of emotional intelligence is to comprehend that an instructor can like you as a person and also give you a low grade based on the quality of your work.

Third, make an appointment to talk with your instructor. Go with a plan! If you did poorly on the midterm or even on the final, ask to take the make-up exam. Ask for a chance to show that you do know the material. Ask if you can write an extra paper or rewrite the project you threw together the night before it was due. Explain why you wish to do better. Instructors are much more inclined to give students a chance when they admit they have done poorly and want to turn things around.

Even if the instructor says you cannot take the test to change your grade, ask to take it anyway to see for yourself if you can do better. Assuming that you will get a better score, this might have a psychological effect on the instructor later.

Most instructors will give you a chance. A bad grade is not inevitable unless you allow it to be. A sincere request for another chance, a specific plan about what you will do, and commitment to do it will influence most instructors.

One of my early learning experiences involved messing up on a mid-term exam. There was no make-up exam. I felt desperate. I wrote out three questions that could be used as the basis for writing long essays. Then I went to the instructor and asked if I could get extra credit for researching and answering one or more of the three questions. I said I would write my answers in the form of a paper using information from outside the textbook. I was delighted when he agreed to my request. I ended up with a "B" in the course. The results would have been different if I had not done the extra credit work. ~ MK

➤ *WARNING:* Do not just walk away from a class where you are doing poorly. Officially drop the class. A failing grade turned in at the end of the course due to non-participation looks bad and becomes part of your permanent school record.

Consider Taking an Incomplete

If you anticipate a bad grade in a course because you have not been able to get all of the work in, and you want to earn a good grade, then consider asking the instructor for an incomplete. Usually, you will have to fill out a form and submit it to your instructor before you can receive an incomplete. All colleges have policies for allowing students to complete course work after the course is over. At most colleges you have at least a year.

Courses Can Be Repeated

You can change the past if you want to. If you get a low grade in an important subject you can repeat the course to replace a low grade with a higher one. Repeating a course is always an option. Some schools average the two grades, some take the higher or more recent.

Instructors Are Human!

Remember, you will have great instructors, average instructors, and some that you believe are teaching only because they couldn't hold a job in the real world. The point is that instructors are human beings who vary in their teaching styles and who react just as you do to the way they are treated.

You can influence the quality of the teaching you get. Here are some practical suggestions, sent to us via the AdultStudent.com website by Barbara Clark, about how to make friends with your instructors and why you should!

> To make the most of your learning experience, and to get the best grades possible, form a positive relationship with each of your instructors. This is easy to do when you are dazzled by the instructor's knowledge. You take opportunities to ask questions, and find yourself encouraged to share your views. An instructor who becomes a mentor helps you make contacts in your field of interest, and coaches you in your early efforts.
>
> Sometimes it is not easy to make friends with an instructor. If the class is large, you can have a lot of competition for the instructor's attention. You may find the instructor's lectures do not address the questions that interest you, or you may notice

that the instructor takes for granted some assumptions that seem questionable to you. Differences in ethnic or economic background can also make it more difficult to build rapport.

If a positive relationship does not come easily, you may feel as though you have to choose between "sucking up" or maintaining your integrity. In these cases you will be aware that you are doing more than half the work of creating any friendship. However, there are good reasons to persevere in this effort. Building alliances with people you do not particularly like is a valuable life skill. It will broaden your horizons to get to know individuals whose point of view is quite different from yours. Think of it as a temporary visit to a very foreign country, where you need to be diplomatic to create cordial relations.

You cannot fake your way into a positive relationship. You still need to show up on time, be well prepared, and think carefully before asking questions or making comments in class. In informal settings, offer information about yourself that might help the instructor find some common interests and remember who you are. Do not criticize, but do let the instructors know in which areas you find their information most helpful.

Getting to know your instructor can improve your grades on class participation and papers, by creating a positive expectation for your contributions. It can even improve your score on multiple choice exams, because you will better understand the instructor's point of view. You can make a game out of predicting which answers the instructor will believe is "right."

In any case, making friends is something you accomplish in small steps. You need not give it a lot of time, but give your full attention to judge what to say. Then notice how it's received. A steady, consistent effort will produce the best results.

Action Review Checklist: Understanding Differences Between Teaching and Learning Styles

◇ When I don't relate to the way an instructor teaches, do I look to see if there is a conflict between my learning style and the instructor's teaching style?

◇ Do I take steps to compensate for my natural preferences in classes with instructors who have different styles?

◇ Have I examined my assumptions about instructors and developed a more realistic and tolerant attitude?

◇ Do I make an effort to become friends with my instructors–even those that I don't like very well?

Action Project for Getting Better Teaching

1. Talk with several classmates about what you like best about instructors. Make a list of specific actions you see as desirable.
2. Make a list of ways you could give positive feedback to an instructor when he or she does things you appreciate.
3. Give instructors positive feedback when they do what you want. Let instructors know what you appreciate.

Learning Team and Support Group Activities

1. Talk about how conflicts between teaching styles and learning styles may be able to explain difficulties you have had with instructors in the past. Work with each other to develop a plan for handling future conflicts.
2. Talk about some of your past experiences with good instructors and poor instructors. Talk about your teaching experiences as parents or managers. How easy is it? What feedback did you appreciate from people you tried to teach?

Send your suggestions! Do you have suggestions about improving relationships with instructors or students? Contact us through the AdultStudent.com website.

Chapter 10

How to Gain Support and Encouragement from Your Family

Do you feel guilty about doing something just for yourself?

Can you ask people for help when you need it?

How do you develop and follow a positive plan of action for getting help and support?

What does it means to give high-quality time to others?

How can you get support that exceeds your expectations?

What rewards can you offer those who give you support?

What can you do if support does not come?

"Who Moved My Life?"

How do you react when someone changes what you expect them to do for you? We all have expectations in our relationships about what others will do and not do. People react to disruptive changes in different ways. As Spencer Johnson portrays in his popular book *Who Moved My Cheese?*, some people adapt very quickly, some change gradually as they see the benefits, and some resist change fearing what they will lose.

Married women report more hassles from their families than single women or married men. There's a lot of pressure on married women to stay in their role of caretaker of the family needs.

Ethel told her support group: "As I was leaving the house Wednesday night, my husband said 'You rushed me through dinner and are leaving me at home alone with the TV to go to that stupid class again? Starting college at 43 is the damnedest thing! Well, go ahead, I'm sure I can amuse myself.'"

Linda, who recently married, said: "My husband has been great. He knows that with a college degree I'll earn more money. He's no dummy. But my mother! Whenever I talk with her, talk about the guilt trip she tries to lay on me. She says 'Why go to college when you could be starting a nice family? It's none of my business, but I want grandchildren. You could have children now and go to school later.'"

Some families go too far, however. Roberto says: "My wife means well, but she treats me like a five-year old starting school. She hovers over me. She interrupts my studying asking can she do this, can she do that? I want her to do what we've always done, not act like Florence Nightingale."

A Plan for Gaining the Support You Need

Fitting into a new role is never easy. It may take six months to a year before you and those close to you make the transition. Here is an effective way to get support, help, encouragement, and understanding from your family and friends:

1. Take some time to think about the support you need from your family in your new role as a student.

2. Be very specific in asking for the support you need—undisturbed time alone, grocery shopping, washing dishes, washing clothes and so forth.

3. Decide to ask for that support.

4. Talk with the people whose support you are seeking. Explain why going to school is important to you. Ask what concerns they might have and listen with understanding. Ask what positive feelings they have about your going back to school and what advantages they may see for themselves.

5. Track positives with people. Reward any actions you regard as positive, helpful, or supportive with thanks and appreciation. Give others immediate feedback about what you like.

Think Ahead

Think through what you want to talk about and what requests you will make. You know your family. Select the best time to have a talk with them.

Taking night classes may mean that the family mealtime will be disrupted. If you are working full-time and going to school part-time, you will have less time together. Use of the family car and your ability to drive them places will change. Find out how they feel about all the changes they will have to adapt to. Empathize with their concerns. Don't tell them not to feel the way they do. Let them know that your time together is important to you and that you want the weeks and months ahead to be a great experience for you all.

If they are reluctant to talk about what is ahead, find a way to get them to think about the months and years ahead. Post a Year-at-a-Glance calendar on a wall with all of your classes marked, your study schedule, and mark dates when you will be doing things together. Using colored pens and sticky notes can make important dates stand out. It is essential to keep the lines of communication open to avoid a big blowup someday at just the wrong time.

◇◇◇

Before I started to school I sat down with the three teenage children who were still at home and talked with them about what changes might occur in their lives as a result of my commitment to school. The kids were wonderful! They encouraged me so heartily I should have been suspicious, but I wasn't.... Years later, after they were out of high school, they told me they were eager to get me involved elsewhere so that they would have more freedom to come and go as they wanted! ~ MK

◇◇◇

Let People Know What You Want

Students with families have requests such as these:

✦ I would like my three teenage children to do more housework, so that I will have more time for my studies.

✦ I'd like my husband and kids to fix dinner for themselves a couple of nights a week when I am at class.

✦ It would be nice to have my wife ask me about my courses and spend a little time talking about my experiences as a student.

✦ I'd appreciate being left alone to study three nights a week; that means not knocking on my door or interrupting to tell me about something on TV.

Why don't adult students get the cooperation they want? The answer is no surprise. They usually have not asked.

Most of us were raised not to be selfish. Some selfishness is essential, however, when expressed in a way that is not demanding.

Most people report that once they have the courage to ask for support, they receive far more than they expected. Some students report that when they finally ask for what they want, the reply is "Why didn't you ask before? Sure, I'll be glad to do that!"

Getting Help at Home

Melinda, an "online mom" with five children, one of them a baby, says:

I enlist the help of my older three children 12, 10, and 8 to help set out breakfast and carry laundry from the machine or empty the dishwasher while I nurse, They will help dress the four-year-old and they love to hold the new baby for brief periods of time.

These things always take time and it is very helpful to have extra hands to do these little jobs.

If you have children, have a cookie and milk or a popcorn meeting with the family each week to develop a responsibility schedule. On a piece of paper, have an older child write down the jobs each person agrees to do and specify when it will be done. Participate in the discussion, of course, but when you have one of the children write down the various duties it will seem less imposed by you.

Post the list in a conspicuous place near your own weekly time schedule. When members of your household see that Thursday evening from 7:30 to 9:00 is a study period, they will be more likely to leave you alone, *especially if you stick with your own schedule!*

Be clear about what you want others to do, ask them to do it, and thank them after they do what you asked.

> *TIP:* Others will be less likely to interrupt or intrude during your study hours if you set aside specific times during the week for each important person.

Quality is Better Than Quantity

Reserve a special time each week for each child. Others will be less demanding when they know they have their own special time scheduled with you.

Melinda, the "online mom" says:
I make it very clear to my children that they are my first priority. I always arrange outside time, a little movie time and private time for homework or reading for each child, usually at the same time, so that none of them is asked to do too much for just me.

Let each child decide what will be done during his or her hour. Self-esteem develops or is maintained by being in close contact with others, by being seen as unique, by feeling important, and from being able to influence the world. So don't plan this hour, let the person influence what you do together.

Be curious about what develops. Many people who have done this report that their personal relationships and contacts with family members improve significantly.

Use a Little Psychology

Thousands of experiments conducted by psychologists over the years have established the validity of principles that affects the actions of others. The principles are:

+ If you reward people quickly after they have done something you like, they will tend to do more.

+ If you don't reward or appreciate people's efforts they will tend to do it less.

Consequently,

+ If you thank, compliment, and reward others for doing what is helpful to you they will do it even more.

+ If you stop rewarding, they'll do less of what is helpful.

What rewards can you use? Here is a list of suggestions from adult students about things they've done:

+ Express appreciation.
+ Say "thank you."
+ Buy or fix their favorite food for them.
+ Give hugs and kisses.
+ Give treats or little gifts.
+ Be interested in their lives.
+ Tell them about something interesting at school.
+ Speak highly of them to others.
+ Give them back rubs and neck massages.
+ Let them feel that your success is their success.
+ Ask what they would like from you.
+ Leave nice notes for them; send cards.

When you speak clearly about what you would like from others and then follow up with "thank-yous" and rewards, you usually get results that exceed your expectations. Most people respond in very positive ways. In fact, you may be overwhelmed by all the love and support others show you.

Melinda says:

When the older children get home from school I have them take turns reading at least three to four books each to the youngest child. Sometimes, I will pay them with coins or a treat to entertain her with a more involved activity, building something, or baking if I have a course deadline. Both bribes work well with them but mostly they are happy to do their share.

Expect Surprises

Expect some surprises and be prepared to make some adjustments of your own when your life changes. Letting people do things their own way may be difficult at first, but a positive attitude and a sense of humor can pull you through.

For example, the grade-school age children volunteered to cook dinner for their college-student mom one evening a week. They accepted full responsibility for shopping, cooking, and cleaning up afterward. Their mother says she assumed the meal would be done the way she always did it. She reports:

The first time they "cooked" dinner they met me at the door all excited and led me to the dining room before I could take off my coat. I expected steaming plates with vegetables, salad, and so forth. When I walked in my eyes almost fell out of my head. Their idea of a great dinner was boiled hot dogs served on paper plates with a bottle of pop, a bag of potato chips, and Twinkies for dessert! I didn't know whether to collapse in hysterical laughter or lecture them on the right way to shop, cook, and serve a nutritious meal. I did neither. As I sat there eating a barely warm wiener, I told myself it wouldn't kill me to let them do it their way. I've had some interesting meals since then. Peanut butter sandwiches and pie aren't too bad. And the paper plates are real time and energy savers.

Adjustments Can Be Difficult

The more your family and friends have been dependent on you, the more difficult it will be for them to be more responsible for themselves. If you meet resistance, the change can be difficult.

They may become upset and refuse to talk. They may accuse you of being selfish and of not caring about them.

There are many reasons for such reactions. A husband may secretly fear that if his wife becomes capable, educated, and employable, she may decide to leave. A wife may feel neglected having her husband work full time and then devote evenings and weekends to school.

Try to not let others make you feel guilty if they become upset. Let them know you understand their feelings but don't take too much responsibility for their unhappy reactions. Would you let a ten-year-old control how you drive or where you go? Are others better qualified to make decisions about your life than you are? Does your partner know your needs better than you do?

Hold true to your plan for yourself while you give others time to adjust to this new way of life. Let them know how important they are to you.

Some adult students find that their home situations do not get better. Some family members may become difficult. A partner may start to drink more or stay out late. Children may begin to get into trouble or have difficulty at school.

If anything this extreme takes place, it is important to seek professional advice and counseling. Get to know what services are available at the college. There are many experts you can talk to and a variety of sources of help. Other students can provide support and practical advice. Ask around and you are likely to discover that more good solutions are possible than you imagined.

Adult students find the return easier if they are prepared for the mixed emotions that others may have about their changed roles. It helps to understand their feelings, and then help them see that your going back to school is good for them as well. You may want to make a list of positive reasons from their perspective.

Going to school can solve problems. Try to use your returning to school as an opportunity to improve your relationship with your loved ones. Healthful relationships are based on people's supporting each other's growth and development, not dependence. Your returning to school could lead to deeper, closer, and warmer feelings of love and appreciation than you ever thought possible.

George was feeling out of touch with his wife, Kathy. They both worked and took classes. It seemed they never talked anymore.

Together they looked at both of their schedules. They made Wednesday lunch and Sunday morning brunch dates top priorities. George says now: "I'd never think of missing one of these dates. That is the time we still know we are in tune with each other and share our triumphs and frustrations. We are back to being best friends."

Include Them

Make your family and friends feel included, not excluded. Try to create the feeling "We are going to college." The more they know about what you do, the more they will understand and support you. A Saturday tour around campus can help introduce them to your new world. Take your spouse or older children to athletic events or concerts. Bring them to the library with you some evening.

Melinda says:

I involve my husband and children as often as I can. I let them know I write about them, which excites them. I've brought home class activities that they feel are "cool." I think the biggest part of my having success is my husband. He is so great about asking what he can do to give me time. I always give him a day or two notice about my deadlines and ask for a block of time (one to two hours) when he gets home. It doesn't always work out, but we both keep trying. Sometimes, it just won't work and I'll have to wait until about 10 PM to get started on classwork and work on through.

My husband also has a lot of experience with colleges that I find helpful to have at home. He can usually answer most of my questions about procedures, he reads my papers, clarifies many issues for me, and is just plain wonderful at giving me encouragement.

Family and friends need to know they are still the top priority in your life. Give them good quality time. Good personal relationships are an essential success foundation as you juggle work, home, and school.

Action Review Checklist: Gaining Support

◇ Have I talked with others about returning to school and how this will affect our lives?

◇ Have I listened well to the concerns and feelings of others?

◇ Have I asked for support in a direct, clear, and specific way?

◇ Can I ask for what I need without feeling guilty or demanding?

◇ Do I tell people frequently how much I appreciate their efforts to help?

◇ Do I have a variety of reinforcements available that I can use to express appreciation?

◇ Have I acquainted myself with all the professional resources available to me at school in case I need advice?

◇ Do I have an active, positive plan for making things work well?

Learning Team and Support Group Activities

1. Talk with each other about what you have done to enlist the support of others. Discuss how it feels to make selfish requests.

2. Help each other find ways to handle challenges. Be sure to tell each other about amusing incidents and your successes.

Chapter 11

How to Balance Going to College with Working

Did you know over 50% of all adult college students work part or full time?

How many credits should you take?

How can you earn college credit by combining work and school?

Did you know that most careers will require you to be a life-long learner?

How can your employers help you accomplish your goals?

You Can Work and Succeed in College, Too

Colleges and employers are adapting to the needs of students who work. Times and locations of where you take your college classes are becoming more flexible. Evening and weekend courses are available. Distance learning and online classes are increasingly available. Some companies will arrange a four day work week so you can take three day seminars or attend weekend classes.

Note also that *you do not have to take all of your courses from the same college!* If a course at another nearby college fits your schedule better or offers courses you need online, you may be able to take that course and transfer the credit. Transferring credit is easy to do between most state-supported colleges.

Course-Load Guidelines

If you work full time, you probably should take no more than two classes in college at one time. The rule of thumb: for every hour of class time, you need two or three hours to do the homework for that class. Thus, if you spend six hours a week in class, you will spend 12 to 18 hours a week in preparation. Add that to a 40-hour work week and you have a major commitment. Travel time from work, home, and school must also be considered. If you are going to school full-time, work should be kept to 20 or fewer hours.

Work-study jobs can allow for split-shift work around class schedules. For some, splitting up school and work is helpful; for others, it is fragmenting. There is no right or wrong way to combine work and school, but there is a way that works best for you. The challenge is to find it.

Employers Will Help You

Employers need educated workers. They need people who learn new technology rapidly, work well as team members, communicate effectively in words and writing, are self-motivated to learn, and can adapt to a rapidly changing work world. In recent years employers have created many ways to encourage, support, and pay for the education and development of the workers they need.

Blending Learning and Working

Most colleges now offer programs for getting college credit for work experience. Credit is offered in a variety of ways that include cooperative education, work-study programs, internships, and practicums.

Cooperative Work Experience

Cooperative work experience allows a student to work and earn college credit while exploring a career choice. When a student has chosen a major such as business, computer science, or engineering, the school's cooperative education department can help arrange work experience in the field.

A student may have a particular job site in mind, or the cooperative work specialist may find an appropriate work placement in the student's major field of study. Specific learning experiences are defined and the student is supervised in meeting the objectives. Co-op students can earns $9,000 per year or more, although some placements are volunteer positions.

Cooperative education supervisors maintain close contact with companies designated as co-op sites. Everything is done to ensure a good learning experience.

It is not possible to receive specific college credit for past employment (except for prior learning credits, see Chapter 3), but you can earn college credit for present employment. If your present work is within the field of your college major, or you are doing certain kinds of work to see if you wish to make it your major field of study, it is worth contacting your cooperative education department to look into the possibility of receiving college credit for your present job.

Work-Study and Student Help

Colleges hire many students to work on campus. The federal government provides funds for the college work-study program. Work-study students qualify for these jobs by showing financial need.

Student-help jobs are also available. They require only that the student is competent to do the work.

Those in the work-study and student-help programs fill in at libraries, locker rooms, receptionists' desks, laboratories, cafeterias, counseling offices, school grounds, and many other college locations. Usually, they work for the minimum wage, but the work experience can be valuable training. It can help clarify career goals and be included on a résumé. These jobs often allow you some study time on the job and your supervisor will shift your work hours to fit your class schedule and exam times.

The recent trend is for more organizations to offer positions to students. They recognize that involving students in work experience is a good way to screen potential employees of all ages. It also helps the work-study student to build job contacts.

Internship Programs

An internship is a training position that may or may not pay you for acquiring a skill while earning college credit. Internships may be offered where expensive equipment or the need for highly trained professionals make on-the-job training cost effective. Prerequisite skills are taught in the classroom, but most of the new learning takes place in the work place.

Two vocational career fields that use many internships are electronic engineering technician and radio/TV broadcasting. These industries grow and change so rapidly that few colleges have the funds or facilities for the latest equipment. Neither can the colleges meet salary scales to hire top people in these fields. A partnership is formed where education experts break the learning process into manageable steps, write the curriculum, assign credit, provide on-site consultation, and see that complementary classwork is provided. Internship programs often lead to a two-year associate degree, or may be a requirement for an advanced degree.

Practicum Training Experiences

Practicum experiences differ from internships in that they often require a year or more of classroom work before a student is allowed on-the-job practical experience. Paraprofessional programs (teaching assistant, legal assistant, and alcohol/drug counselor) have significant practical experience as an essential part of the vocational degree program.

On-the-job training may take anywhere from three months to more than a year. This practicum training is coupled with classroom discussion and job supervision. (Note: students rarely receive payment for practicum experience. The personal supervision you receive from experts is valuable compensation.) Some schools may have an on-campus clinic where practicums can be completed.

Balancing Predictable School and Work Demands

Many jobs have peak demand periods. In retail sales, the pre-Christmas weeks are the busiest time of the year. In school, it's mid-terms and finals. For college support services, fall registration is a busy time.

When your work times are predictably busy, lighten your school load to accommodate them. Get papers done early and read ahead in your textbook. Talk with your instructor about doing work early—or get an approved delay, if needed. When you have to juggle work and school, knowing how to use your options is a survival tool.

College, Work, Family, Friends, and Time For You

Many adult students are successfully using the guidelines and suggestions in Chapters 9 and 10. It *is* possible to combine going to college with studying, family life, working, and still have time for yourself.

Many students find that when they organize their time better, ask others for help or understanding, and work only on the most important things to be done, they can accomplish much more than they ever thought possible. Many students find that a small personal organizer, sometimes used with a "Palm" type personal digital assistant, or Blackberry, greatly increases how much they can get done in the time available. As we've said before, you don't have to be an extraordinary person to succeed in college. All you have to do is be in control of what you do with yourself.

➦ If you do not have specific career goals or personal life goals, read the "Developing Goals" article at our website: AdultStudent.com

Also, make sure to talk with counselors in the careers center at your college. There is a wealth of helpful information available.

Action Review Checklist:
Balancing Work and School

◇ Do I have a realistic school and work schedule?

◇ Have I explored the possibility of getting college credit for work experience?

◇ Have I asked my employer about ways that my educational efforts could be paid for or reimbursed?

◇ Have I asked my employer for flexibility around my class schedule and examination periods?

◇ Have I worked out a schedule for working, attending classes, studying, family and recreational time?

Learning Team and Support Group Activities

1. Do the members of your group work? What sort of balance between work and study have you each arranged? What do you know about ways to work for pay, earn college credit, and gain on-the-job experience?

2. Compare your work, class, study, and family schedules and discuss how well they are working. Share any tips or suggestions you've found helpful.

Chapter 12

How to
Handle Pressures Well

What is the difference between stress and strain?

Do you believe the way for your life to get better is for other people to change?

How can some stress can be good for you?

Can you be both optimistic and pessimistic?

What is the "good child" handicap?

How can you decrease your negative experiences and increase your positive experiences?

How to Handle Pressure and Strain

Some people deal with pressure better than others. You probably have several friends or acquaintances who are very durable and resilient. They cope well with life's difficulties. You probably also know several people who can turn an ordinary day into a tragedy.

This chapter will show how to hold up well under the many pressures that can build up when you have to attend classes and study while you handle other important responsibilities, work, and raise a family. Before we look at practical ways to increase your resiliency, however, we need to clarify some misunderstandings about stress.

Stress has received a bad name in recent years. Many people think stress is bad. It isn't. *Too much* stress may be bad for you, but a certain amount is necessary for health and well-being.

Dr. Selye Made a Mistake

Much of the misunderstanding about stress traces back to Dr. Hans Selye, the physician who created the concept *biological stress* in 1936. After decades of writing and speaking about stress, however, he apologized in his memoirs for using the wrong term. He explained that when he came from Europe to attend medical school he did not understand either the English language or physics very well. He said his research was about strain, not stress. He said he should have named his concept the *strain syndrome.*

There Is No "Stress" In Any Situation Until a Person Experiences Strain They Don't Like

In physics a stressor is an external force attempting to deform an object. The effect on an object is measured as strain. What is a mild strain for one person can be extreme stress for another person in the same situation.

Many People Blame the Situation for Their Reaction To It

It is not unusual to hear people claim that they have stressful jobs, stresses at home, or stresses as college students. That is a misperception. They are confusing the situation with their reaction to it. It isn't the circumstance itself, it is your reaction to it that counts. What is distressing for one person is an easy workout for another.

An instructor that one student complains about for being extremely tough is appreciated by another for setting high standards.

Stressful Situations Can Be Beneficial

Dr. Selye coined the term eustress ("good stress") to emphasize that everyone needs a certain level of stress. When we work at handling the strains we face, we gradually get stronger. Athletes build up their physical strength with frequent workouts. Professional training programs build competence by straining people to their limits. Emotionally stressful experiences can motivate people to learn new coping skills. Some mothers, for example, handle the addition of a fourth child to their family more easily than they handled having their first child.

Stress Resistant Personalities

Two people in an identical situation will have different reactions to it. Some mothers enjoy talking about their amusing experiences raising a family. Other mothers are so distressed trying to raise their families they need tranquilizers, counseling, and emotional support.

The situation a person is in is not the problem. *It is how a person deals with a situation* that explains why some people become sick while others become strong in identical circumstances. The following list summarizes the research findings about persons less likely to develop stress related illness. As you read the list check to see how well it describes you:

+ rarely feel upset during events in routine activities;
+ feel capable of taking effective action about upsetting events;
+ draw action choices from a wide range of inner and external resources;
+ experience family and friends as caring and supportive;
+ manage self-change well; and
+ convert negative experiences into beneficial learning.
+ become stronger, better and wiser every year.

Recognize the Signs of Not Coping Well

Indicators that the pressures are getting to be too much include: sleepless nights, increased alcohol consumption, losing your temper over a minor incident, migraine headaches, frequent colds and illnesses, auto accidents, ulcers flaring up, high blood pressure and other cardiovascular problems, losing track of time, falling asleep in class, and forgetting to bring a paper you stayed up late at night to finish.

How to Cope Effectively With Lots of Pressures

For most adult students, the challenge is not having to deal with one major difficulty, the challenge is how to hold up week after week handling a whole lot of little things.

It is important to avoid feeling helpless and at the mercy of external forces. Here is a practical plan of action for decreasing emotional strain while increasing your hardiness and resiliency.

Decrease the Pressures

1. *Make a list of everything you experience as negative, upsetting, or stressful.*

   Sometimes the only way to be more positive is let yourself be negative. When you make a list of everything you feel pressured about, you are not a negative person, you are an emotionally healthy person taking the first step toward coping well. Recognizing all the forces working against you is the first step for preparing to deal with them.

2. *Express your feelings about your list.*

   It is not unusual to experience some physical and emotional upsets when you start college for the first time. Forgetfulness, stomach and intestinal problems, and sleeping difficulties are normal reactions to stress. These symptoms are usually temporary and should diminish quickly if you find outlets for your feelings.

3. *Go through your list, item by item, asking questions:*
   + Can I do something about this? How direct is my contact?

✦ What if I ignored this or avoided contact?

✦ Can I change the situation in some way? Who could help me?

✦ What if I changed my reaction to it?

The aim is to find ways to minimize the impact of the entire list. It isn't usually one big thing that does a person in, it is the accumulation of many little things. With this plan you diminish the effects of too many strains, avoid feeling helpless, and increase feelings of control.

◇◇◇

Although I'm a pretty relaxed person most of the time, I did learn to recognize when stress was building up. I finally figured out that from time to time I would develop this overwhelming urge to clean the house, which meant that I was feeling too much pressure. I knew that things were really bad when the urge to clean the house changed and became specific—*I wanted to clean the refrigerator!* ~ MK

◇◇◇

Increase Positive and Revitalizing Experiences

1. *Make a list of things you experience as positive in your life.* Ask yourself what activities make you feel happy and relaxed. What makes you feel good? Reflect on pleasant experiences.

2. *Ask questions about how to repeat, increase, or have new positive experiences.*

   ✦ Am I ignoring or taking for granted some positive aspects?

   ✦ What do I enjoy doing? What do I get enthusiastic about?

   ✦ What would I like to do that I keep putting off?

   ✦ Who do I enjoy sharing good experiences with?

3. *Do several things that make you feel good and are good for you.* It is important to be self-nourishing even though it may look like selfishness. Psychologically healthy people are both selfish and unselfish. They act in ways that are good for their well-being while still being helpful to others.

Revitalizing Activities

Laugh and Play With Friends

Successful students do not study all the time. Do anything you can to prevent your college life from getting too serious, too burdensome, and too heavy. Make a conscious effort to get into activities where you can laugh or play hard and completely forget your responsibilities at school, home, and work.

Stay Physically Active

Do something, anything, several times each week that works your muscles. This might be bike riding, gardening, jogging, racquetball, tennis, swimming, or fast walking. It may be a yoga class. In any case, activities that work your muscles keep you healthy and help you sleep better, which in turn will help with your schoolwork. If you are not doing much of this now, take another look at the recreation facilities on campus.

Take Naps, Meditate, or Listen to Music

Naps are a wonderful way to relax and revitalize yourself. If you have a car at school, try taking naps in your car. Take a short nap early in the evening instead of watching television before studying. Take naps on weekends if you wish.

Research into meditation shows that it has many beneficial effects. Find a place where you can sit and do nothing for a few minutes each day. Don't use the time to solve problems. Focus your attention on a beautiful scene. Recall one of your most enjoyable vacations. Take easy, relaxing breaths. Most counseling centers have useful books, CDs and DVDs on how to increase relaxation and reduce stress.

Another option is to sit and listen to classical music while doing nothing else. Sit back and totally lose yourself in the music. The word "music" means something that enhances musing. So do it.... Muse....

Overcoming the "Good Child" Handicap

Your self-esteem influences how well you do in college and in life. Many people were trained by their parents to never brag or praise themselves. As a result, they never develop a healthy level of self-esteem. It takes courage to defy old parental prohibitions, but it must be done to achieve and enjoy success.

Without strong self-esteem you will probably find it difficult to even imagine getting a high grade point average. Your expectations and actions are controlled by worries about what others might think. You are afraid that if you got top grades others would think that you think you are superior to them.

Self-esteem is your opinion of yourself. Strong self-esteem is like a thick emotional skin. It acts as a buffer to shrug off hurtful criticisms. When someone is critical, your self-esteem lets you decide that you like *your* opinion of yourself better than theirs. Self-esteem lets you appreciate compliments. It determines how much you learn after something goes wrong.

> ➤ *NOTE:* Self-esteem is strengthened by positive self-talk.
> Make a list of all the things you like and appreciate about
> yourself.

The actions outlined in this chapter will decrease feelings of pressure, increase revitalizing experiences, and increase your ability to do well in your courses. It is a simple, effective plan that will increase your hardiness and resiliency.

If you were raised to be a "good girl" or a "good boy," told to never be prideful, never be negative, and never act in selfish ways, the coping plan will be difficult. Your parents had good intentions. But trying to go through life acting like a good five-year-old is a handicap in a constantly changing world.

Mentally healthy people can list what they are unhappy about, can make requests of others, and include themselves on their list of people they do nice things for. Here are some things to consider doing for yourself:

Becoming Stronger and More Hardy

✦ The ability to handle sustained pressure over a long period of time can be learned. An effective plan of action includes reducing negative, distressing experiences while increasing positive, revitalizing experiences.

✦ By seeing that a stressful experience is an experience of strain that you don't like, you avoid feeling victimized. You can use strain like a workout at a fitness center. Consciously engage each strain, then pause briefly before engaging the next one. Just as bike riding, jogging, or swimming leads to getting physically stronger, using emotional strains as workouts leads to becoming mentally and emotionally stronger.

✦ Remember, it isn't the situation, it is your response to it that counts. What is distressing for one person is not stressful for another. When you take steps to cope with pressures and negative experiences, you will experience less stress and strain. Martha Washington once observed:

> I am still determined to be cheerful and happy in whatever situation I may be, for I have also learned from experience that the greater part of our happiness or misery depends upon our dispositions and not upon our circumstances.

Action Review Checklist: Handling Pressures Well

◇ I have listed all the things I experience as negative, and developed plans for reducing, changing, avoiding, or minimizing them.

◇ I have listed what is positive and revitalizing for me and have a plan for increasing my pleasant, revitalizing experiences.

◇ I am able to consciously like and appreciate myself.

◇ I understand the feeling of distress is emotional strain and that strain can lead to getting stronger and better.

◇ I am getting better and better at handling pressure.

Learning Team and Support Group Activities

1. Talk about the pressures you each feel. Ask each other "How do you manage?" Find out what you each do that is enjoyable, positive, and revitalizing.

2. Discuss your reactions to reading that an important step toward thriving under pressure is to list everything you feel negative about. Was it difficult to express negative feelings?

3. Talk about how you might have been raised to be a "good child" who never complains, is not selfish, and has low self-esteem.

4. Discuss how easy or difficult it is to engage in activities that may seem selfish. How have others reacted when you've acted in selfish ways? Discuss your feelings about developing strong self-esteem.

5. Did a disruptive change such as job loss or divorce lead to your enrolling in college? If so, how well have you dealt with your feelings about this matter?

Chapter 13

Resiliency in a World of Non-Stop Change*

How are curiosity, playfulness, intuition, and humor are related to resiliency?

How can you learn useful lessons from everyday experiences?

What are your three inner "selfs" and how can you strengthen them?

How many paradoxical traits do you have?

What are the steps for converting misfortune into good luck?

* This chapter adapted from Al Siebert's book,
  The Resiliency Advantage

Resiliency Makes the Difference

Jackie Leno Grant felt out of place as a Native American in a nearly all-white high school in rural Oregon. When she skipped classes, the administrators sent her to a school for delinquents. Her unfair treatment could have made her bitter and rebellious, but Jackie studied hard and never got into trouble. She graduated with good grades, got a job, and enrolled in a community college. She earned a college degree and became a college advisor working with minority students.

What is Your Response to Adversity?

How do you react to life's difficulties? Do you react like a victim or do you respond by coping and learning from the difficulty?

The victim reaction is to be crushed by the blow. The victim habit is to complain: "This isn't fair!" "They've ruined my life." "Look what they've done to me." People with victim patterns focus backward on the past and blame others for their unhappy circumstances.

Highly resilient people respond to adversity by learning and coping. When hurt and distressed they expect to find a way to have things turn out well.

Resilience is the ability to sustain good health and energy under constant pressure, cope well with high levels of ongoing, disruptive change, bounce back from setbacks, overcome adversities, and work in new ways—without reacting like a victim or acting in dysfunctional ways. Resilient people adapt quickly and have a talent for making difficulties work out well.

Suzy Kellett, for example, gave birth to quadruplets when she was 31 years old. Her husband couldn't deal with four new born babies and walked out. He left her in their Idaho home to cope with the four infants by herself, with no help, and no income to pay the rent and other bills.

Suzy telephoned her parents in Illinois. They volunteered to take them all into their home, so she packed up their few belongings and flew to Chicago—with nearby passengers on the flight helping to hold the infants. Everyone felt sorry for her. People would have understood if she had drifted into self-pity, complained how unfair life had been to her, and blamed her husband for her plight. But Suzy says "I never allowed myself to wonder how my life would be if I only had one baby. I knew that wouldn't be productive. I had the fabulous four. I had to accept what was real."

Suzy says her humor helped her be resilient. Today her four children are college educated, starting their own lives, and she has a great job as a director of a state office that helps film makers. Looking back on the entire experience, she says "there were tough times, but I'd do it again because the good far outweighed the bad!"

Life's best survivors get better and better with age. Like cats, they manage to land on their feet when the bottom drops out of their lives.

Resilience is Essential in Today's World

To remain healthy and cope well, everyone must be able to deal with unexpected challenges and overcome adversities. Highly resilient people know how to bounce back from setbacks and find a way to have things turn out well. They thrive in non-stop change because they are optimistic, flexible, and creative. When hit by major setbacks they don't complain about life being unfair, and often end up stronger and better than before.

Everyone is born with the capacity to develop resiliency abilities. The five levels are:

1. Optimize Your Health and Well-Being
2. Focus Outward: Good Problem Solving Skills
3. Focus Inward: Develop Strong Inner "Selfs"
4. Develop Excellent Resiliency Skills
5. Develop a Talent for Serendipity

The first level of resiliency is to sustain your health, your energy, and positive feelings. (How to do this was covered in Chapter 12.)

The second level of resiliency is based on research findings that outward looking, problem-focused coping leads to resiliency. The least resilient people focus on their emotions and may become so emotional it interferes with good problem solving by others.

You've probably heard that many psychologists are referring

to the human cerebral cortex as being divided into the "right brain" and "left brain." This description comes from research showing that the two halves of the cerebral cortex function in very different ways.

The *left-brain* approach to problem solving is rational, logical, and follows a linear step-by-step process. It works like this:

1. *The first step is to accurately understand the nature of the threat, challenge, or difficulty.* You accomplish this by privately asking questions such as: What is the problem? How serious is it? How urgent is it? How much time do I have? What information do I need? Is this a problem I can do anything about? Must I be the one who takes action?

2. *Ask yourself "What do I want?"* What is my goal? What kind of outcome would satisfy me? Does it take into account the needs of everyone who would be affected?

3. *Outline two or more possible ways to overcome the problem.* Then look at the risks and potential negative effects of each of your solutions. If you have time, it is very useful to discuss the possible solutions with a friend, colleague, or mentor. A sign of your emotional intelligence is your ability to ask for opinions about ways that your plans and strategies won't work.

4. *Take action.* It is normal to feel a bit anxious because you will be doing or saying something that you have never done before. When you know exactly what to do about a difficulty, it isn't a problem!

5. *Look at the effects of the action you have taken.* At this step you ask questions aimed at getting accurate feedback. If you are working on a problem that will take a long time to resolve, then look for small indications that things are moving in the right direction. In organizations it can take weeks and months to reach a satisfactory resolution of a problem.

6. *Learn from the feedback you get.* Reappraise your understanding of the problem and the situation.

7. *Modify your efforts.* When what you are doing isn't working, do something else!

8. *Is the outcome satisfactory to you?* Can you now leave the situation alone and move on to other things?

9. *Ask yourself what you learned from this.* Were there early clues that you ignored? What were the lessons here for you? How can you avoid having to deal with a similar problem again in the future?

Some problems can't be handled with the rational, left-brain approach. *Right-brained*, creative, intuitive problem-solving can be a better way to find an unusual, solution that works. You start by asking yourself many questions to free your imagination from the restrictions of "normal" thinking and assumptions. You have probably heard the phrase "thinking outside of the box." It takes uncensored questions to break out of the invisible walls of socially-approved thinking to let your imagination soar free.

Here are some examples of questions that can lead to a creative solution. Be playful in imagining various things you might do. Allow yourself some private, outrageous thoughts. Creative breakthroughs often come after some far out thinking:

✦ What is the real problem here? Am I sure?

✦ What would be a different way to describe what is happening?

✦ What would be an unusual solution?

✦ What if I did the opposite of what is usually done?

The question is, can you use both left-brain and right-brain methods when trying to solve problems? If you don't, you are limiting your resiliency options. As was said by a city planner taking a resiliency class, "two brains are better than one!"

Develop Strong Inner "Selfs"

The third level of resiliency focuses on the inner roots of resilience: self-confidence, self-esteem, and self-concept. These three "self's" like like invisible gatekeepers that control your access to a vast range of personal talents, abilities, and attitudes that emerge at the fourth level of resiliency. If you support your gatekeepers, they will support you. If they are weak or undermined by you, they will handicap you.

Here are ways to strengthen your inner gatekeepers:
Strengthen Your Self-Confidence. Self-confidence refers to how well you expect to do in new situations. It is an action predictor. Think of self-confidence as your reputation with yourself. People with strong self-confidence expect to succeed in new activities and overcome unknown adversities. People with weak self-confidence resist trying new activities. People with strong self-confidence know they can count on themselves even more than they can count on anyone else.

To increase your self-confidence, make a list of all the things you've done well. Describe what you know you're good at doing. Ask yourself "What are my reliable strengths and abilities? What do I do well?"

Strengthen Your Self-Esteem. Self-esteem is your emotional opinion of yourself. It is how you feel about yourself as a person. Self-esteem is like a thick emotional blanket that buffers you from hurtful criticism and insensitive comments from others. Self-esteem makes up the gap between positive feedback you receive from others and what you need to psychologically sustain yourself. If you were raised to be a "good child" you may think that praising yourself or accepting compliments is a sign of pridefulness or that you think you are better than others, but that isn't true. False modesty is an act that attempts to manipulate what others think of you. It is an act that many people can see through.

How do you develop stronger self-esteem? Make a list of all the ways you value yourself and feel good about yourself. It is very important to be able to consciously appreciate yourself. If you feel reluctant to do such a list, this is a sign that you really need to do it!

Strengthen Your Self-Concept. Self-concept refers to your idea about who and what you are. Inner attributes that you value will be unchanged by a change in job status, income level, where you live, or marital status. One way to strengthen your self-concept is to identify with being a resilient person. Do you think of yourself as being resilient? Think of experiences in your past that were rough on you, but that you managed to overcome. It may help to keep in mind that the greater the difficulty faced, the greater the inner strength, ability, and wisdom that can be gained from the struggle to master it. Remember: If you develop a self-concept of being resilient, you automatically give yourself more strength for handling even the roughest situations.

These three core "self's" are like gatekeepers to your higher level abilities. These three body-mind "selfs" are functions of the somatic, autonomic, and central nervous systems. As you gain more and more life experience, you develop each of them in a way that is effective for you. People with weak gatekeepers are not very resilient. If the gatekeepers are strong and healthy, you can access and develop many fourth-level resiliency strengths.

Child-Like Curiosity is a Resiliency Skill

At the fourth level of resiliency you fully develop the attributes and skills found in highly resilient people. These include being very curious, having a playful sense of humor, and frequently learning valuable lessons in the school of life.

To handle change or a disruptive situation well, you must read the new reality rapidly. You must quickly and accurately understand and comprehend what is happening.

Being open to read, assess, and respond to new developments is a reflex in people who adapt faster and better than others. It is a brain habit based on retaining a child-like curiosity throughout one's life.

Do you ask lots of questions? Wonder how things work? Wonder how and why other people do what they do?

This sort of curiosity gives a person a mind that quickly comprehends upsetting developments and changes that bewilder others. People who thrive in a changing world are accustomed to what is unusual, complicated, and mysterious. That is why, when hit with disruptive change and unexpected difficulties, they quickly absorb information about what is happening.

Playful Humor Makes a Big Difference

Threats and crises can trigger a "freeze, fight, or flee" reaction. A strong surge of adrenaline can increase the speed of your muscular reflexes and your muscle strength, but it impairs good problem solving. That is why laughing or joking during a crisis is very practical!

Why does humor help? Laughing reduces tension. Creative problem solving, accurate thinking, and good physical coordination are best in moderate emotional states. Alan Alda's irreverent humor as Hawkeye in the television series "*M.A.S.H.*" was an excellent example. He was serious about being a surgeon but not about being a soldier. Hawkeye's sense of humor is typical of people who are best at dealing with emergencies and dicey situations.

The humor is not hostile or hurtful. It is directed toward the situation. The person toys with what is happening and pokes fun at it. Chances for surviving are increased by the attitude, "I am bigger than this situation. This is my toy. I am going to play with it."

Humorous playing is a way of asking "How does this look from a different point of view? What would happen if I turned it upside down? What if the reverse were true? What unusual things exist here?" By playing and toying with the situation, the person avoids being overwhelmed and at the same time is likely to come up with a way to survive.

How about you? Have you ever been poked in the ribs for muttering a humorous comment during a serious moment? If so, that is a good sign.

Change Requires Learning

If you look in an introductory psychology textbook you will find that "learning" will usually be defined as "A relatively permanent change in behavior that results from experience."

Do you see the point? Change and learning go together. You can't have one without the other. Learning leads to change; change requires learning.

When faced with life or job changes that no parent or teacher prepared you for, you must manage your learning by asking questions and finding your own answers. To react to life as a school means to ask questions such as:

"Why did they do that?", "What is the lesson here for me?", and "What do I need to do differently now?" The ability to learn valuable lessons from bad experiences is a high level resiliency skill. Here are the steps to follow:

1. Ask "What happened?"
2. Replay the incident as an observer.
3. Describe what happened. Put it into words.
4. Ask "What can I learn from this? What is the lesson here?"
5. Ask "Next time, what will I do differently?"
6. The next time a person says that to me, what will I say?
7. Imagine yourself handling the situation well the next time.
8. See and feel yourself getting the outcome you desire.
9. Rehearse the effective response.

When you follow these steps for self-managed learning, you will increase your self-confidence and look forward to the next incident with positive anticipation. In contrast, a person who dwells on a past experience with anger and distress anticipates the next incident with dread and does not expect a good outcome. This is why whatever you expect to happen, whether good or bad, usually determines the way things turn out.

Become Very Good at Learning in the School of Life

We humans are the only creatures on earth that must learn how to interact effectively with the environment we are born into. Other creatures are born with their brains "hard-wired" to interact with the environments they are born into in neurologically programmed ways such as to find food, avoid danger, and co-habit with their own species.

But what happens when the environment that supports a species changes? Wildlife biologists say that when a species' environment changes, there are three possible outcomes: It will adapt, migrate, or die. This is why environmental changes are causing so many species to die out. They do not have it in them to learn new ways of existing in new environments. We humans, in contrast, can keep learning new ways to survive and thrive in new environments all our lives. A great advantage of being a human being is that we can replace old behaviors with new behaviors at any age.

It's useful to understand that you were born with the ability to learn in three different ways. The first kind of learning is emphasized when children are sent to school. What they learn is scheduled and controlled by teachers. School is a teaching environment. Teachers are evaluated on how well their students do on various tests.

A second kind of learning comes from imitating effective people. From role models we acquire the action patterns of others.

The third way is self-motivated, self-managed learning. It is the learning that comes directly from your own experience. Life is a learning environment for people who learn on their own. In the school of life, a skilled student can learn useful lessons from rough experiences.

Here's another way to look at the differences in how people learn: When you take classes in a school, first you learn the lesson and then you take a test. In the school of life, first you take the test and then you learn a lesson. Highly resilient people learn in all three ways. They learn in classes, learn from role models, and learn useful lessons on their own.

Abraham Maslow is quoted as saying that no one achieves full self-actualization until the age of sixty. He saw that people who constantly learn from life's experiences get better and better decade after decade.

Your most valuable learning comes from lessons you learn in the school of life. Throughout this book, whenever we addressed a difficult situation, our approach has been to show you that no matter what happens, you have the inborn ability to handle the difficulty in a new way that makes you a stronger, more capable person.

Be Adaptable and Flexible

Survivors of extreme adversity say that the two most important qualities in survival are the ability to be flexible and adaptable. A person must be able to do something different than they ever did before, perhaps even the opposite.

What makes inner flexibility possible? Counterbalanced personality traits. They let you be both one way and the opposite, both pessimistic and optimistic, for example.

Can a person be both? Yes. Life's most resilient survivors are comfortable with their paradoxical qualities even though the popular thinking is that people are either one way or the other, such as either pessimistic or optimistic.

Paradoxical or counter-balanced personality traits are something like having both extensor and flexor muscles in your arm. You can make your arms, hands, and fingers do what you want because you control the choice point between two sets of opposing muscles.

How flexible and paradoxical are you? Look at the two lists below. Check off the traits you possess. Add traits not listed in the spaces at the bottom or on a separate page.

❑ calm	❑ emotional
❑ trusting	❑ cautious
❑ strong	❑ gentle
❑ serious	❑ playful
❑ lazy	❑ hard-working
❑ stingy	❑ generous
❑ curious	❑ indifferent
❑ self-confident	❑ self-critical
❑ pessimistic	❑ optimistic
❑ unselfish	❑ selfish
❑ _____	❑ _____
❑ _____	❑ _____

If you looked at the lists and quickly decided "All of the above, depending on the situation," that's wonderful. If you wrote down several more pairs of paradoxical or contradictory qualities you've noticed about yourself, that is an excellent sign.

It is important to understand that the lists are not meant to be a comprehensive listing of all possible pairs. The two lists were created to demonstrate an important point. Being paradoxical gives you flexibility and the more pairs of paradoxical traits you have, the more flexible you are at dealing with any situation that develops. If you identify with having many such contradictory traits you will have many more pairs than those listed.

Having opposing personality traits is like having a reverse gear in a car. It lets you back up when you need to. People without many counter-balanced or paradoxical pairs of traits are emotionally handicapped. They are rigid and inflexible because they were trained to be one-sided. They were taught to never be selfish, negative, angry, lazy, or self-appreciating.

One-sided people are difficult to live and work with. They have an energy draining effect on work teams. They are so concerned about acting as they think they should, they interfere with things working well.

It is also true that some people have so many contrary qualities they are flaky. They have an energy draining effect on work teams because they are emotionally scattered and disorganized. The key factor is to always remain focused on having things work well for yourself and others. In a workplace, highly resilient people are more effective than others because they interact with what is happening in ways that lead to things working well for everyone. They have mastered the art of allowing things to work well. They are the "go to" people when something essential must be done right.

Practice Intuition and Empathy

The people who thrive in a variety of situations trust their intuition and have good empathy skills. They monitor their own internal emotional state and can read the emotional states of others as well.

Coping with new situations often depends on a sense that something is wrong. A tight stomach or an uneasy feeling may be the clue. These feelings can be set off by anything—a person's tone of voice, something not said, a group's quietness, anything at all that doesn't fit.

Women are usually better than men at using intuition because most women are raised practicing it. Men who practice intuition can develop the same ability, however, because it is based on subliminal perception—something that exists within every human.

People who handle others well are able to step out of their own feelings and views to empathize with the feelings and perceptions of others. People most likely to be successful in job interviews start by conducting interviews about the organization they would like to work for. A company won't hire you because you need money to pay your bills. They may hire you if you can present yourself as having skills they need.

Empathy does not mean you are a weak, easily hurt bleeding heart. Survivor empathy is the kind Abraham Lincoln used during his years as a defense attorney. He was very successful because he would begin his opening statements to the jury presenting a better case against his client than the opposing attorney was prepared to do.

Empathy includes understanding people who live and think in disliked ways, including people who forced you to have to be resilient. The attitude of the empathy described here is "whether I like you or dislike you, I am going to understand you as well as you understand yourself—and maybe better."

Level Five Resiliency: Convert Misfortune into Good Fortune

You may have heard the word serendipity. Horace Walpole coined the term to describe a person having the wisdom to see that an accident or unfortunate development is actually a stroke of good fortune.

Your talent for serendipity comes from asking questions such as "Is there anything good about what has happened?" "Is there a gift here for me?" "What problem does this solve?"

Perhaps you have heard someone say that losing their job, getting cancer, or being divorced was one of the best things that ever happened to them. Can you look back at a rough situation and appreciate that it was also good for you?

We humans have the ability to find value in bad experiences

and convert misfortune into good luck. The better you are at thriving, the more you will avoid reacting to disruptive change like a victim and can find the joy of serendipity in rough situations.

Resiliency Principles:

✦ Resiliency is not something a person is either born with or not, resiliency is a life competency that is gradually learned.

✦ Becoming more and more resilient requires feeling personally responsible for learning ways to handle tomorrow better than yesterday.

✦ Life isn't fair, and that can be very good for you. When hit by a major life disruption, you will never be the same again. You will emerge either stronger or weaker, either better or bitter. Resiliency comes from a proactive decision to find ways to overcome adversity. The struggle to bounce back and recover from setbacks can lead to developing strengths and abilities you didn't know you were capable of.

✦ As you struggle with adversity or disruptive change, your mind and your habits will create either barriers or bridges to a better future. Blaming others for how bad things are for you keeps you in a non-resilient, reactive, victim state in which you do not learn conscious resiliency responses.

✦ Your unique resiliency strengths develop from self-motivated, self-managed learning in the school of life.

✦ The observing place in you is where you develop response choices about ways to interact effectively with the world you live in. Choices lead to feelings of freedom, independence, and being in control of your life.

✦ As you become more and more resilient, you effectively handle disruptive change, adversities, and major setbacks better, faster, and easier.

Action Review: How Resilient Are You?*

Rate yourself from one to five on the following:

(1 = very little, 5 = very strong)

___ Very resilient. Adapt quickly. Good at bouncing back from difficulties.

___ Optimistic, see difficulties as temporary, expect to overcome them, and have things to turn out well.

___ In a crisis I calm myself and focus on taking useful actions.

___ Good at solving problems logically.

___ Can think up creative solutions. Trust intuition.

___ Feel self-confident, enjoy healthy self-esteem, and have an attitude of professionalism about work.

___ Curious, ask questions, want to know how things work, experiment.

___ Playful, find the humor, laugh at self, chuckle.

___ Constantly learn from experience and from the experiences of others.

___ Very flexible. Feel comfortable with inner complexity (trusting and cautious, unselfish and selfish, optimistic and pessimistic, etc.)

___ Anticipate problems and expect the unexpected.

___ Able to tolerate ambiguity and uncertainty about situations.

___ Good listener. Good empathy skills. "Read" people well. Can adapt to various personality styles. Non-judgmental (even with difficult people).

___ Able to recover emotionally from losses and setbacks. Can express feelings to others, let go of anger, overcome discouragement, and ask for help.

___ Very durable, keep on going during tough times. Independent spirit.

___ Have been made stronger and better by difficult experiences.

___ Have converted misfortune into good fortune, found an unexpected benefit.

═══════════════════

___ Total Score

Scoring: Over 75 —highly resilient!
 65-75—better than most
 55-65—slow, but adequate
 45-55—you're struggling
 45 or under—seek help!

An explanation of the items can be found by visiting: www.ResiliencyQuiz.com

Learning Team and Support Group Activities

1. Describe from your own experience the difference between people who thrive well in difficult situations and people who can turn an ordinary day into a horrible experience.

2. Describe the difference between people who bring an attitude of professionalism to their work and people who are qualified, but have an unprofessional attitude. How do group members deal with unprofessional attitudes?

3. Talk with each other about your reaction to learning it is desirable to have paradoxical personality traits. Were you raised to be one way but not the opposite? Trained to be a "good" child?

4. Tell each other about one of the worst experiences of your life and what you learned or gained from it.

Resources and Selected Reading

Chapter 1

Dweck, Carol. *Mindset: The New Psychology of Success,* New York: Random House, 2006.

McClelland, David C., and David G. Winter. *Motivating Economic Achievement.* New York: Free Press, 1969.

Seligman, Martin E.P. *Learned Optimism,* New York : A.A. Knopf, 1991.

Chapter 2

Bob DePrato quote from *Your Hidden Credentials,* by Peter Smith. Washington, DC: Acropolis Books, 1986, p. 67. An encouraging book for adult students.

Eva Corazon Fernando-Lumba quote from *The Oregonian,* May 30, 1991.

"Findings from the Condition of Education: Nontraditional Undergraduates" report NCES 2002–012, National Center for Education Statistics, 2002. PDF available online.

Sher, Barbara, and Annie Gottlieb. *Teamworks!* New York: Warner Books, 1991. Contains valuable guidelines for forming and running a support group.

Chapter 3

Burd, Stephen. "The student-loan scam," *The Los Angeles Times.* April 10, 2007.

"The Clark Howard Show," WSB Radio, Atlanta. Consumer Advocate Clark Howard offers practical advice and tips on how to avoid being scammed. Podcasts available at: www.ClarkHoward.com.

Cuomo, Andrew M. "Testimony: United States House of Representatives, Committee on Education and Labor," April 25, 2007. Plus additional press releases at the State of New York Office of the Attorney General website.

Ekstrom, Ruth B., Abigail M. Harris, and Marlaine E. Lockheed. *How to Get College Credit for What You Have Learned as a Homemaker and Volunteer.* 1988. Princeton, NJ: Educational Testing Service.

Foundation Center. *Grants for Minorities.* New York: Foundation Center, 2003-2004 (updated regularly). www.FoundationCenter. org. Also check this site for grant info for students with disabilities, women and more.

Go to The Associated Press (ap.org) or United Press International (upi.com) website and search on "student loan." You will be directed to the most current information presented by the press.

Hechinger, Grace. "Will Your Company Pay for Your Classes?" *Glamour Magazine,* Feb. 1987.

Two book on sources of money for adult students are *Guide to Getting Financial Aid* and *The Scholarship Book.* Updated yearly by the College Board. Be sure to explore www.CollegeBoard.com which is a great source for other useful information.

US Department of Education. *Funding Education Beyond High School, 2008-2009* (updated annually). Free PDF file: http://studentaid.ed.gov/students/publications/student_guide /index.html

US News & World Report financial aid (also check their excellent education section)*:* http://www.usnews.com/sections/business /paying-for-college/

"29 lenders subpoenaed in scrutiny of student loans." *USA Today,* Oct. 25, 2007.

USAToday.com. "College tuition and fees up more than 6% at four-year public schools." Oct. 24, 2006 (Accessed Feb. 22, 2008).

Chapter 4
Edna Mae Pitman quote from *The Oregonian,* Jan. 1989.

Chapter 5
USAToday.com. "New answers for eLearning." Jan. 10, 2008 (Accessed Feb. 22, 2008).

Chapter 6

Lakein, Alan. *How to Get Control of Your Time and Your Life*. New York: New American Library, 1989. A classic book. Lakein shows how to establish priorities for yourself, choose activities that are of highest value to you, and minimize the amount of time you put into low payoff activities. Your school may have a copy of the video or dvd based on this book. If so, you can arrange to preview it. Take a few friends.

Adelizzi, Jane Utley, and Diane B. Goss (Eds.). *A Closer Look: Perspectives and Reflections on College Students with Learning Disabilities*. Milton, MA: Curry College Press, 1995. A free copy of this book in MSWord format is available at the Curry College website. Look for the "Publications and Outreach" link from the Program for Advancement of Learning (PAL) page at: http://www.curry.edu/Academics/LD+Program+(PAL)/

Chapter 7

Bloom, B.S. (Ed.). *Taxonomy of educational objectives: The classification of educational goals: Handbook I, cognitive domain,* (1956). New York; Toronto: Longmans, Green

McKeachie, Wilbert J., Donald Pollie, and Joseph Speisman. "Relieving Anxiety in Classroom Examination." *Journal of Abnormal and Social Psychology*. Vol. 50, No. 1, Jan. 1955, pp. 93-98.

Chapter 8

Strunk, William, Jr., and E.B. White, *The Elements of Style, 4th Ed*. Mineola, NY: Dover, 2006. Valuable to anyone wanting to improve the quality and clarity of their written communications. It shows how to use good grammar, punctuate correctly, and write clearly.

Chapter 9

Chapman, Elwood N., and Sharon Lund O'Neil. *Your Attitude Is Showing, 12th Ed*. New Jersey: Prentice Hall, 2008.

Keirsey, David. *Please Understand Me II*. Del Mar, Calif.: Prometheus Nemesis Book Co., 1998.

Kolb, D.A. *The Learning Style Inventory: Technical Manual.* Boston: McBer, 1976.

Hays, Pamela, and R. Ellis. *Communication Activities for Personal Life Strategies.* Dubuque, Iowa: Kendall/Hunt Publishing Company, 1989.

Murray, Bridget. "Professor's Most Grating Habits." *Monitor on Psychology,* American Psychological Association, Vol. 31, No. 1, Jan. 2000, pp. 56-57.

Chapter 10

Johnson, Spencer, MD. *Who Moved My Cheese?* New York: Putnam, 1998.

Mendelsohn, Pam. *Happier by Degrees.* New York: Dutton, 1980. Practical advice for women in college who have families. Covers how student mothers become better mothers; how husbands and children react and think; being a single parent; and advice from husbands of college students to other husbands.

"Taking Charge" and other articles on "How to Reinvent Your Life," *Modern Maturity,* Jan/Feb, 2000, pp 26-45.

Chapter 11

Directory of College Cooperative Education Programs. Edited by Polly Hutcheson. National Commission for Cooperative Education, Phoenix: Oryx Press, 1996. Check the website for a current listing of Co-op Education publications and resources: http://www.co-op.edu/

Transition to Work program sponsored by the Adaptive Learning Division of Foothill College: http://www.foothill.edu/al/ttw.html

Northeastern University Coop Education: http://www.coop.neu.edu/

Chapter 12

Colgrove, Melba, PhD, Harold Bloomfield, MD, and Peter McWilliams. *How to Survive the Loss of Love,* Los Angeles: Prelude Press, 1993.

Flach, Frederic. *Resilience: How to Bounce Back When the Going Gets Tough.* New York: Hatherleigh Press, 1997.

Siebert, Al. *The Survivor Personality*. New York: Berkeley/Perigee, 2010.

Siebert, Al. "Promoting Resiliency: Encouraging Employees to Thrive Under Adversity," *The EAPA Exchange*, National Employee Assistance Professionals Newsletter, Jan/Feb, 2002, pp. 15-17.

Chapter 13

This chapter is adapted from *The Resiliency Advantage,* by Al Siebert. San Francisco: Berrett-Koehler Publishers, Inc., 2005.

Kipplinger Washington Letter, December 22, 1999, "Your education won't stop when you leave high school or college. You'll be a life-long learner—classes at night, at work, or on the Net.... You will rely more on your own wits and resources for success than previous generations. Employer and government safety nets will shrink."

Aitken, Sandi, and John Morgan. "How Motorola Promotes Good Health," in *The Journal For Quality and Participation,* Jan/Feb, 1999, pp. 54-57.

Day, Laura. *Practical Intuition for Success.* New York: HarperCollins, 1997.

Pulley, Mary Lynn, and Terrance E. Deal. *Losing Your Job—Reclaiming Your Soul: Stories of Resilience, Renewal, and Hope.* Jossey-Bass, 1997.

Rubin, Bonnie Miller. "Secrets of Resilient Women," *Good Housekeeping,* January, 2000, pp. 108-111.

Ury, William. *Getting Past No: Negotiating in Difficult Situations.* New York: Bantam Books, 2007. A practical book on how to develop empathy for opponents.

Read more about Jackie Leno Grant and Suzy Kellett in the "Past Stories of the Month" file at THRIVEnet.com.

Online Resources

The following internet sites provide a small sample of the vast amounts of useful information for college students found on the internet. Much of what we've listed are not-for-profit or educational organizations. We included some commercial listings with useful and accessible information. A more comprehensive listing of links can be found at:

> http://www.adultstudent.com/student/slinks.html

Adult Student Resources
AdultStudent.com
> http://www.adultstudent.com

About.com Adult Education
> http://adulted.about.com

Adult Student Center
> http://www.adultstudentcenter.com

Association for Non-Traditional Students in Higher Education:
> http://www.antshe.org

Back2College:
> http://www.back2college.com

College Level Examination Program:
> http://www.collegeboard.com/clep

General College Resources
Sites such as magazines, newspapers and television stations often have education sections and resources for college students. Try Newsweek.com, USNews.com and USAToday.com as starters.

US Department of Education:
> http://www.ed.gov

College Board Online:
> http://www.collegeboard.com

Education Index (provides student reviews of colleges):
> http://www.educationindex.com/

Making College Count:
> http://www.makingcollegecount.com

Financial Aid Resources

US Dept of Education, financial info:
> http://studentaid.ed.gov/guide

Cash for College (a Free PDF file):
> http://www.nasfaa.org/SubHomes/Cash4college/index.html

College is Possible (American Council on Education):
> http://www.collegeispossible.org

FastWeb (a FREE scholarship matching service):
> http://www.fastweb.com

FinAid (free tips on finding financial aid):
> http://www.finaid.org

Sallie Mae (largest provider of federal student loans):
> http://www.salliemae.com

Strategies for the Non-Traditional Student:
> http://www.freschinfo.com/strategy-nontrad.php

Resources for Students with Disabilities

Foothill College Resources for Students with Disabilities:
> http://www.foothill.edu/al/drc.php

Program for Advancement of Learning (from Curry College):
> http://www.curry.edu/Academics/LD+Program+(PAL)

National Center for Learning Disabilities:
> http://www.ncld.org

Distance Learning Resources

Listing of US University websites:
> http://www.utexas.edu/world/univ/state/#toc

Distance Education Clearinghouse (Univ. of Wisc.):
> http://www.uwex.edu/disted/

Distance Education Frequently Asked Question Archive:
> http://www.faqs.org/faqs/education/distance-ed-faq

Portfolio

Portfolio Library:
> http://www.amby.com/kimeldorf/portfolio

Texas Tech School of Mass Communication:
> http://www.depts.ttu.edu/masscom/programs/career
> /resume.php

Career Search / Basic Job Resources

4Jobs.com:
> http://www.4jobs.com

America's Job Bank / Career OneStop:
> http://www.jobbankinfo.org

Occupational Outlook Handbook:
> http://www.bls.gov/oco

Career Builder:
> http://www.careerbuilder.com

Employment Guide:
> http://www.employmentguide.com

MonsterTRAK (Monster.com for College Students):
> http://www.monstertrak.com

Jobweb (Nat'l Assoc. of Colleges and Employers):
> http://www.jobweb.com

National Commission for Cooperative Education:
> http://www.co-op.edu

The Riley Guide: Job Resources on the Internet:
> http://www.rileyguide.com

Amby's Work Site:
> http://www.amby.com/worksite

Miscellaneous / Study Help

CampusCalm:
> http://www.campuscalm.com

How-to-Study.com:
> http://www.howto-study.com

Self-Help Counseling Center, University of Buffalo:
> http://ub-counseling.buffalo.edu/selfhelp.html

Study Skills Self Help:
> http://www.ucc.vt.edu/stdysk/stdyhlp.html

Study tips from UC Berkley:
> http://slc.berkeley.edu/studystrategies
> /acadsuccess_resources.htm

Test Taking Tips:
> http://www.testtakingtips.com

Sample Searching Keywords:

Use the following keywords alone or in combination at your favorite internet searching site for additional adult student resources: adult college student, adult learner, college financial assistance, college funding, college money, campus counseling center, continuing education, distance learning, financial aid, grants, nontraditional student, re-entry student, returning student, scholarships, student success, student orientation, study help, study resources.

Searching Tips:

+ *Use the "back" button on your browser,* or alternately, the "History" or "Go" menus. This will come in handy if you performed a search on a search engine and want to get back to the list of returned sites with out having to type in the search again. Also, opening search result links in a new window will keep your results page available in the background. Beware of "Back" buttons on a web page. They may not take you "back" to where you expected. You can also choose to open resulting sites in a new window or tab.

+ *Use a multi-search engine to start:* Dogpile.com, Metacrawler.com, Excite.com or similar are good ones to try. They will search a number of other search engines for their top matches. You may get duplicate listings, but you'll get a feel for which engine is providing you with the best matches for your query. If you want more listings from any one search engine, you can then visit the ones that have the most relevant data.

+ *Browse the search engine's directory:* Most search engines not only allow you to search the web for your term, but have already categorized listings of sites related to your question. Check the "Education" category on Yahoo.com, for example.

+ *Explore the sites you visit.* If you find a single page article that has useful information on it, take the time to explore what else the site offers. Hit their Home Page link, or "backstep" as described below in "404 FileNot Found."

✦ *Use the site's built-in search engine.* Many sites incorporate their own on-site search engine. These are very useful for finding the specific information you might be after. Use your browser's "find" command to search for a term on the page you're browsing. This is useful on a page with a lot of content. Sometimes you'll find the on-site search is not very good. You can use the Google,com engine to search the content of any site by typing "site:www.examplesite.com" (for example) in the window before your search terms.

✦ *Server busy error:* This usually indicates that the server (a computer "hosting" the file or site) you're wanting is either temporarily not functioning, overloaded, or the pathway to the server is obstructed somehow. Try to access the site at a later time.

✦ *Unable to locate a server:* This usually means that the server is no longer in service, that you made a typing error, or the address wasn't quite right. Sometimes, though, the big routing servers go down and computers from a certain region may not be able to "find" the address you want to go to. Try again later or check whether the domain name (server name) is valid. Do this by visiting http://www.whois.net/ for a "who is" searching gateway. You can type in the domain name and it will return a screen that tells you if and to whom the domain name has been registered.

✦ *"404 File not found" error* when trying to access a site means that the server is working, but that the specific file is no lon-ger available. Sometimes the owner of the file has changed services or reconstructed the site. If the owner has moved, you will have to search for the title of the file on a search en-gine. If the site has been reorganized, you may be able to find the file you want by backstepping the cursor in the address line deleting the characters back to a "/" mark and hitting "en-ter" again. Keep doing this until you get to a spot where a real page or directory listing is displayed and look for the file you want. Don't be discouraged by "directory listing denied" er-rors, that's just good internet security.

Index

Acknowledgements

We wish to express our special thanks to:

Timothy L. Walter for his many contributions to the original, first edition of this book.

The students and instructors who critiqued previous editions and provided us with valuable feedback.

Lonna Liddell for her information about Prior Learning Assessment programs.

Wilbert J. McKeachie and the University of Michigan psychology department faculty for creating a climate of professionalism in teaching.

John Gardner, Stuart Hunter, and the other Freshman Year Experience staff (past and present) at the University of South Carolina for their dedication to first-year students and their excellent stewardship.

Theresa Kappus, Distance Services Librarian, Gonzaga University, for her suggestions for updates to our library section.

Our families for their constant support and appreciation.

About the Authors

Al Siebert is Director of The Resiliency Center, and author of the award-winning *The Resiliency Advantage: Master Change, Thrive Under Pressure, and Bounce Back From Setbacks,* and *The Survivor Personality: Why Some People Are Stronger, Smarter, and More Skillful at Handling Life's Difficulties...and How You Can Be, Too.* He received his MA and PhD in psychology from the University of Michigan on the GI Bill. He taught adult education classes for over 35 years and is author of several "Student Success" books. He is internationally recognized for his knowledge into the nature of highly resilient survivors and is quoted in many books and magazines. He has been interviewed on National Public Radio, the *NBC Today Show, CNN, OPRAH,* and more.

Mary Karr started college when the youngest of her four children started high school. She earned a BS in psychology and speech communication and her MS in speech communication. She teaches a college success seminar for re-entry students, and created and taught several online communication courses for Marylhurst University.

Feedback Request

Please let us know how you did! In what ways was *The Adult Student's Guide to Survival and Success* helpful to you? How was having a success group beneficial?

Do you have any suggestions on how *The Adult Student's Guide* could be improved? Write to us in care of:

Practical Psychology Press
PO Box 535
Portland, OR 97207

press@thrivenet.com

www.PracticalPsychologyPress.com

Complete our online survey for a chance to win a copy of Dr. Siebert's *The Resiliency Advantage: Master Change, Thrive Under Pressure, and Bounce Back From Setbacks* given away quarterly:

www.AdultStudent.com/survey

Instructors:
Download our accompanying Instructor's Manual, *Teaching College Success to Adult Learners* at:
www.AdultStudent.com/eds/im

Also Available

Books:

THE RESILIENCY ADVANTAGE: Master Change, Thrive Under Pressure, and Bounce Back From Setbacks, Al Siebert, PhD
Berrett-Koehler, 2005. (Winner, 2006 Independent Publisher's Best Self-Help Book) ISBN: 978-1-57675-329-3

THE SURVIVOR PERSONALITY: Why Some People Are Stronger, Smarter, and More Skillful at Handling Life's Difficulties... and How You Can Be, Too, Al Siebert, PhD
(Foreword by Bernie Siegel, MD)
Berkley/Perigee Books, 2010. ISBN: 978-0-399-53592-5

Order online at:
PracticalPsychologyPress.com

Satisfaction guaranteed.

For other books, resources, and an online eCourse about survivor resiliency, visit our sister website at:

ResiliencyCenter.com